Teaching Dogs Practical Life Skills
A Step by Step Practical Guide & Workbook

What to Teach ~ How to Teach It
When to Teach It

By Meesh Masters of
The Dog's Point of View
Force Free Teaching with Empathy, Compassion & Understanding

Photography By
Jonathan Hall

Disclaimer

Everything written and explained within this book has been designed to teach using Force Free and positive reward based methods. Nothing within these explanations or exercises should distress or cause your dog to become anxious in any way. If you notice your dog becoming agitated or distressed, stop immediately and reassess how you're applying the exercises, and if you have followed the process without rushing or expecting too much from your dog too quickly. If you're in any doubt, please consult a force free professional.

If your dog already has existing behavioural issues such as reactivity or any form of aggressive or guarding tendencies, I recommend you consult a force free professional to help you in the early stages, to make sure both you and your dog learn in the best way possible for you both. There is a list of recommended professional bodies to source your force free trainer from at the back of the book.

Success with these exercises is absolutely achievable, as has been proven by their application with both in person and online teaching clients. I cannot, however, make any guarantee's for you and your dog, without being able to work with you personally and oversee the application of your teaching & your dog's learning processes.

Dedication

To all the dogs I've had the great privilege of sharing my life with
To all the dogs and their families I've had the great privilege of working with
I owe you all so much

Each and every one of you have made me a better student,
a better teacher and a better person.
May we all meet again one day.

With Thanks To...

My Son for his love and belief in me always

My family and close friends, for their unfailing support & encouragement

All the amazing trainers and specialists I've had the great privilege to learn from

TABLE OF CONTENTS

FOREWORD 1

It's Not 'Just' a Dog 2

SECTION 1: TEACHING DOGS - THE ESSENTIAL ELEMENTS 3

    #1 - If you're not doing this, don't expect your dog to either 3

    #2 - How long will it take for your dog to be 'trained' 5

    #3 - The big picture 8

    #4 - Why doesn't your dog do as you ask even though they know what you mean? 9

    #5 - How to make teaching your dog as easy as possible 11

    Things that can impact on learning and behaviour 15

    The teaching and learning process from the Dog's point of view 21

    Positive Brain Focus 23

    How will you help your dog choose you? 23

SECTION 2 : PRACTICAL LIFE SKILLS STEP BY STEP TEACHING GUIDES 32

    Marker Method of Teaching 32

    Lead Techniques 36

    Hand Signals 40

    Conditioned Name Response 42

    Voluntary Check In 49

    Voluntary Close / With Me 54

    Loose Lead Walking (Foundation Exercises) 58

    This Way 67

    Proofed Sit 72

    Impulse Control 77

    Leave it 82

    Let's Go 91

    Touch 95

    Recall 101

    Emergency Stop 112

    Settle 119

    Over 125

SECTION 3 : WHICH TEACHING GUIDES DO YOU NEED & WHEN 129

    For Dogs That Ignore You 129

    For Dogs that Lack Self Control 130

    For Dogs that Pull on the Lead 131

    For Dogs that don't Come When Called 131

    For Dogs that Chase Things 132

    For Dogs that Jump Up 133

    For Dogs that like to Bark a Lot 134

    For Dogs that Can be Reactive on Walks 135

FINAL THOUGHTS 137

ABOUT THE AUTHOR 138

APPENDIX 140

    Essential Elements Action Worksheets 140

    References 148

    Resources 148

FOREWORD

As you can imagine, being someone who is passionate about helping dogs and their families live happy, enjoyable and problem free lives together, my ultimate goal is to be able to help as many people as possible.

The number one reason why dogs are dumped, abandoned or surrendered to rescue shelters is due to behaviour problems, and the sad fact is, that most of these dogs were simply dogs being dogs doing what dogs do. They didn't do anything 'wrong' per se, but their behaviour was inappropriate for the human environment they were living in, and things got bad enough that their family felt they could no longer deal with it.

From working with my clients, and the feedback I've had from them, I wanted to provide easy to understand and workable solutions, that don't require a scientific degree in canine psychology to understand (that's my passion not yours.) If I can help and support people and their dogs as they work through their problems to achieve mutually beneficial outcomes, then I could literally be saving lives. Once in the rescue system, many dogs sadly end up with more emotional and behavioural issues and therefore greater difficulty finding forever homes.

As much as my aim is to make solutions easy to understand and apply, that doesn't mean there's no work involved, of course there is. As with any relationship, you have to work at it, you have to be committed to it, and you have to bring your patience and compassion into it. Hopefully, if I can simplify the process for you, by explaining how to see things from the Dog's point of view, and then provide you with the information and tools you need to be able to confidently teach your dog, then it will reduce confusion and create successful outcomes for you both.

This book is obviously not a be all and end all teaching guide, that would be a very big book! What I hope I have put together here, is a structured way to approach some everyday practical life skills for dogs and puppies that, when taught and practised, can help you and your dog enjoy a deeper understanding of each other. By helping you develop a strong bond, and find a way to effectively communicate with each other, the end result is you get a well behaved dog, your dog gets to enjoy more freedom and you both get to have more fun.

Where emotionally based problem behaviours are concerned, things like fearfulness, guarding or reactivity, there's obviously a lot more to deal with. However, many of the exercises in this book are required, and indeed form the foundation for the emotional rebalancing techniques that will solve these problems.

Knowledge is confidence. When both you and your dog know exactly what to do and when, your behaviour becomes confident and your communications clear, which means your dogs behaviour will be consistent, instead of acting on impulse or reacting from a lack of better choices available to them.

It's Not 'Just' a Dog

We are not our dogs masters... we don't own a dog... we are in a relationship with our Dogs.

And as with any relationship we enter into, there has to be understanding, clear communication, compromise at times, boundaries, empathy and of course trust and mutual respect. Imagine what a human relationship would look like without those things?

Now don't go thinking for one second I'm saying dogs are like humans, or dogs are small furry people, thankfully they really are not! However, something that's becoming more and more mainstream these days in the world of teaching dogs and behavioural understanding, is that dogs are far more complex than we previously understood.

'Your Dog is a Thinking, Feeling, Emotional Being
Just Like You... But Different'

By realising how much the world, situations, experiences, family dynamics, genetics, stress, ill health, pain, environmental change and a whole host of other day to day living experiences can affect our dogs far more than we knew, it makes it easier to see how problems can arise. It enables us to do what's needed to ensure we educate, acclimatise, habituate and empathise to help our dogs feel relaxed, confident and safe living in the human world with us.

By helping pet dog guardians realise why this happens, or why their dog did that, I hear time and time again things like, 'ohhhhh right, that makes perfect sense now'. With that understanding, they find it easier to make slight changes to what they do, which in turn has a totally different impact on what their dog does. Many clients report they don't feel like they're 'training' but more like they have improved their ability to communicate with their dog, which of course means their dog understands them better.

Although the exercises we use to 'train' our dogs, including those here in this book, are described and viewed as 'dog training', for me, it's not really about 'training' at all. It's about what and how we communicate and interact with our dogs day in day out within the construct of our daily lives together, which is the key foundation to any successful relationship.

You wouldn't dream of having a child without being prepared to spend many years providing them with the social skills, education and emotional well being to grow into a confident, well adjusted human being, and the same is true of welcoming a dog into your home. Whether you choose a puppy, a rescue dog, a purebred pedigree or a mongrel, be prepared for at least 18 months to 2 years of education and then ongoing maintenance of those skills. Yes, it will require you to spend some time focused on teaching, but not as much as you might think, and the effort you put into those first couple of years, no matter what age your dog is, will pay dividends back tenfold in the life you get to share together thereafter.

SECTION 1
Teaching Dogs - The Essential Elements

Enjoying a happy, stress free life with dogs is not just about teaching them, it's about enjoying the relationship you have with them. They deserve to be part of the family, but some of the things dogs love to do are not always appropriate in a human world.

So, just like if you were to go and live on an alien planet, your alien teachers would have to educate you about that world. What is acceptable behaviour, what isn't, how to enjoy your life there, do the things you love to do and have fun but without putting yourself in danger. How to connect with your alien family, even though you don't speak the same language, so you can have a mutual respect and understanding of each other and live in harmony together.

And this is our duty to our dogs...

Although there are many ways to teach a dog how to do particular behaviours, personally I feel there are 5 essential elements, that encompass all aspects of teaching dogs how to live happily alongside their human family members, without squashing their beautiful spirits, but at the same time without them causing havoc in our homes and lives!

Essential Element #1
If You're Not Doing This, Don't Expect Your Dog to Either

One of the easiest ways to end up with a dog that SOMETIMES does what you want them to, but not always, and usually not at the times you really want them to, is to be inconsistent.

Consistency is for me, the #1 Essential Element, because without it, even if you're doing all the others, it's likely that things will still not end up as reliable as you want them to be, because the ultimate result of inconsistency, is a dog that doesn't clearly understand what you want from them.

Let's look at a couple of examples....

If you have a dog that pulls on the lead, and you would like to change this behaviour so they walk nicely on the lead beside you no matter where you are, then you have to be consistent with YOUR behaviour when teaching them. If you sometimes allow them to pull, even just for a few metres at a time, they're not getting a clear and distinct communication that walking relaxed on a loose lead is the behaviour you want, because sometimes, from your Dog's point of view, it's ok to pull.

So to allow them to pull, albeit with less intensity at times, creates confusion for your dog as to what is expected of them, and ultimately makes teaching them to walk nicely on a loose lead take waaaaaaay longer!

The same applies to behaviours like jumping up, if this is a behaviour you're trying to stop your dog doing, it has to apply to everyone they meet. It's not fair on your dog to allow them to jump up at some people and not others, they're not going to understand the rules of 'It's ok to jump up at Uncle Bert, but you mustn't jump up at Auntie Bettie' ... and then you tell them off for jumping up at Auntie Bettie.

In this scenario, it would be better to teach your dog to do a calm sit when visitors come, then teach a fun 'Jump Up' behaviour using a specific word, for those people who are happy for your dog to do that, but they have to stay calm first, or sit, and then be INVITED to jump up, go crazy and have fun. ☺

Dog's find this type of communication and consistency easier to understand and therefore it builds confidence & reliability, because they know what's expected of them. Let's face it, we ALL love it when we get it right, and the same is true for our dogs.

Another area where inconsistencies pop up quite a lot, is in the words you use to communicate to your dog. It's quite important and will help you get better results if you, and everyone else, uses the same words for the same behaviours. If you can imagine you're trying to learn a new language, and they have 4 different words that all mean the same thing, it's going to get pretty confusing for you.

I often hear 4 or 5 different words used when asking for the same thing. You're walking along, your dog is ahead of you and you want them to stop for whatever reason. For this I've heard...

- Stop
- Wait
- Hang on
- Dog's Name (with no further instruction)

Or your dog is barking and you'd like them to stop. For this I've heard...

- Quiet
- Shush
- That's enough
- Stop it

Another area of confusion for our dogs can be when we use the same word for lots of different things. For example the word DOWN used to ask a dog to:

- Lay down
- Get down when jumping up
- Get off the sofa
- Get out of the car

You can see how this could be pretty confusing for them. So if there's something you're struggling with, stop and take a few minutes to consider if YOUR behaviour and the way you're teaching is consistent, looking at it from your Dog's point of view.

Consistency

- ✓ Makes it easier for your dog to learn

- ✓ Makes it easier for you to teach, because you develop consistency in YOUR behaviours

- ✓ Makes it easier for your dog to generalise their behaviour to other locations/situations

- ✓ Makes it easier for your dog to respond correctly

- ✓ Makes it more likely your dogs behaviours will be reliable & they will respond when it matters

- ✓ Is less stressful for your dog and you ☺

Essential Element #2
How Long Will it Take for Your Dog to be 'Trained'

So this is a question I get asked a lot!   How long will it take...

- For my dog to be 'trained'
- For my dog to have a reliable recall
- For my dog to stop misbehaving
- For my dog to walk nicely on a lead
- For my dog to be ok around other dogs
- etc etc etc...

The thing is, there are so many variable to take into consideration, it's literally impossible to say. To name just a few, there are things like...

- ? How old your dog is

- ? What breed your dog is

- ? Your dogs character

- ? Your dogs base level emotional state, and by that I mean is your dog naturally fearful, anxious, confident

- ? Your dogs history

- ? What sort of relationship you have with your dog

- ? What yours and your dogs daily lifestyle is like

- ? How much time you have to focus on practising with your dog

- ? If your dog has any established habits

Did you realise there were so many?

BUT before you go getting all despondent, and feeling like you will never achieve that kind of connected and in tune relationship with your dog that you've always dreamed of, there are quite a few simple things you can do, that could have a super positive impact.

This actually leads on from Essential Element #1, which is why it's #2! Funny huh? I can sum up these first two elements in one sentence for you to easily remember ...

One of the most powerful influences over your dogs behaviour
is YOUR behaviour

So what is the 2nd component? It's habits! Both yours & your dogs. Do you know how powerful habits are?... And remember, good habits are just as powerful as bad ones, so, all we need to do is strengthen those good habits (both yours & your dogs) and weaken the bad ones right?

Cool, easy yes?

Hmmmmmm it is and it isn't, have you ever tried to change a habit you have? I bet it wasn't as easy as you thought, and there's a very good reason for that, so don't beat yourself up, like I just said, habits are powerful!

But that can work in our favour too, so read on to find out how looking at, and changing a few of your habits, and in turn your dogs habits, could have a very positive impact on your dogs general behaviour.

The reason habits are so powerful is because they're historically repeated automated behaviours. Our brain likes to take things we do a lot, over and over, and put them on autopilot in the unconscious area of our brain, to save time & energy, otherwise we would literally get overloaded with things to do and think about. Things like brushing your teeth, changing gears in a car, locking your front door on your way out are all the kind of automated behaviours that you do so often, you rarely think about them, even to the point (if your anything like me) sometimes you have to check you've done them, because it felt like you didn't! That's the power of habits.

So how does this help you with your dogs behaviour?

By looking at some of yours & your dogs everyday habits, you can make slight alterations that could change the outcome of what happens. Now it's not really possible for me to say which habits would be best to look for, because I don't know what niggly little problems you put up with every day with your four pawed family members.

Remember these are just alterations to your current habits or reactions to your dogs behaviour. You still need to do the teaching required (in the absence of triggers) to actually affect these behaviours in a more long lasting & positive way, but changing your habitual response will help move that process along quicker. So I'm just going to leave a little list here to give you the idea.

Example list of habits that could negatively influence your dogs behaviour

Your Dog's Behaviour	Your Behaviours Negative Influence
Your dog pulls on the lead	You keep walking & let them Maybe you pull them back
Your dog barks out the window	You get cross & shout at them
Your dog jumps up at you when you come home	You tell them off, push them away
Your dog begs at the dinner table	You talk to them, maybe give them something
Your dog reacts barking at other dogs	You tighten the lead when you see other dogs & try to pull them away

Example list of NEW habits that could positively influence your dogs behaviour

Your Dog's Behaviour	Your New Behaviours Positive Influence
Your dog pulls on the lead	You stop You reward them whenever they are by your side
Your dog barks out the window	You acknowledge they have alerted to something You redirect them onto a game/chew toy
Your dog jumps up at you when you come home	You ignore any 'rude' and excitable behaviour, but as soon as they're calm you praise & make a fuss of them
Your dog begs at the dinner table	You ignore your dog when you're eating You never feed them from your plate
Your dog reacts barking at other dogs	You focus on your behaviour, you proactively create distance on sight of another dog, belly breathe & focus on keeping the lead soft using practised lead techniques

I've included a blank copy of the Habits Action Worksheet at the end of this book, to help you get started.

One of the most difficult things about changing a habit, because of how they work, is REMEMBERING you want to be doing something different to what you normally do. So I've got you covered there as well, with some really quick & easy ways to remind yourself of what you want to be doing instead, and I've included it in your Habits Action Worksheet at the end of the book.

Essential Element #3
The Big Picture

This 3rd Essential Element is one that most people don't realise, or forget to think about, especially when working to change a problem behaviour. *(Remember though, they're only problem behaviours to you, to your dog, they're just behaviours.)*

So the thing is, if you don't take this element into consideration, then as with the other two, even if you're doing everything else right, it could be having a negative effect on your teaching efforts.

Let's take, as an example, a reactive dog that barks & lunges at other dogs when they're out walking on a lead (it's an ever increasing problem I know.) What most people do, including some trainers, is get started straight away trying to address that behaviour as quickly as possible.

Whilst this is not wrong, as long as it's approached the right way, a possible problem with this approach is that it's likely the behaviour is not a standalone problem, and this can apply to lots of other behavioural issues as well.

It's important to give some thought to the big picture and take into consideration, any and all other things that may be going on, that could be having an impact on this particular behaviour.

To start with, the example I used above is an emotional response, not just a behaviour that can be 'trained' into something different, so it needs to be addressed differently anyway, but that's a whole other topic that I will be covering in a lot more detail in an online course that will be available soon.

The bottom line is, if you have a problem behaviour, or are trying to teach your dog a new behaviour, but there are other things going on that are negatively affecting your dogs ability to do what you're asking him, then THAT behaviour is working against you constantly. So you can see why it might take you longer to achieve progress and ultimately a successful outcome.

There are some examples below of what I mean, and yep you guessed it, I've got a printed sheet already made up for you (which you can find in the Appendices section at the back of the book) to help you determine if there are other things you need to look at with your dogs behaviours, in relation to solving any problems you may be having.

Behaviour Problem	Big Picture (Other behaviours that could be negatively impacting)
Fido is reactive on walks	Fido also pulls on the lead Fido also has no self control around visitors Fido also barks a lot at noises outside the house
Fido Jumps up at visitors	Fido also has no self control around food Fido is also hyperactive a lot of the time Fido whines a lot & wants your attention
Fido pulls on the lead	Fido is also hyperactive at home a lot of the time Fido also ignores you a lot out on walks Fido also chases fast moving objects (traffic, bikes)
Fido is destructive when left	Fido also follows you everywhere when you're home Fido also barks a lot at things outside Fido also has noise phobias (fireworks, thunderstorms)

What's important to remember here, is that there could be several things in the big picture having a negative impact, so it can help to be aware of all of them, enabling you to determine which can be managed for the time being if necessary, and which really need to be worked on alongside the main problem, to make sure you can make great progress.

The good thing is, as you work on each one, it can have a positive knock on effect on some of the others ☺

Essential Element #4
Why doesn't your dog do as you ask even though they know what you mean?

Your dog knows what 'Sit' means, but they won't do it when you meet someone on the street?

They get all excited and leap all over them! Your dog knows what 'Here' means, but sometimes they just ignore you and carry on sniffing, or worse, run off to say 'Hi ' to other people or dogs, as if you don't even exist!

How annoying is that! Why does that happen?

Here's why, most people start teaching their dogs, and get to a point and think they're done, because their dog comes back 'most' of the time, or is fairly good at staying with them on walks (unless they see something interesting) or will usually sit when told. So their dog responds 'mostly', and they believe they now know that behaviour, and are 'trained'.

Then what happens is, when their dog doesn't respond at the crucial times they need them to, they label them deaf, stubborn, stupid or even dominant, because they 'know' how to do it... but don't!

It's sooooo frustrating right?

The thing is, although your dog may know what you're asking of them, they don't necessarily know how to do it in ALL situations. Dogs do not generalise in the same way we do, what this means is, just because your dog will come to you at home, in the garden or on your local familiar walk, it doesn't mean they will do it all the time anywhere. It doesn't mean they will do it when there are other people across the park, or there's another dog nearby, or children playing with a football.

You have to PRACTISE your teaching in lots of different contexts for the behaviour to become reliable. At home, in the garden, on the street, at the park, on a busy field, in the town centre, at the local woods etc, you get the picture.

Obviously not all the behaviours we want our dogs to learn are relevant to all of those kinds of places. You wouldn't take your dog to the town centre and practise recall for instance, but you may take them there to teach them how to sit quietly in a busy environment (once you've done the teaching exercises for this). So take a moment to think about the kinds of places you want to go with your dog, and the kinds of situations that you want & need them to respond in, then, once your dog knows the basic behaviour well, you have to **deliberately** seek out those particular environments and practise in them.

It sounds a lot of work, but it actually isn't in reality, if you approach it the right way. Once your dog has learnt a behaviour, although it needs to be practised in all these different contexts and places, they actually progress much quicker each time, because muscle memory is building up and the behaviour is becoming more of a habit (remember those habits we spoke about) which means they learn faster.

The reason it may feel like it takes a long time, is when you DON'T practise in different locations and situations, because every time your dog fails to respond, you're starting to undo the teaching you have done so far, so you're constantly in this yoyo place where it feels like 2 steps forward and one step back.

Yes it does take a bit of proactive thinking, and a degree of focus and commitment on your part, but isn't that worth it to have a well behaved, happy, confident dog you can take all the places you want to? Once it's done, it's pretty much in there for life (with a little maintenance of course.)

I wanted to give you a couple of examples to get my point across, BUT I don't want you to feel overwhelmed by this, and feel like teaching your dog is going to be a constant full time job! That's not the case, and I'll be covering how to make it as easy and quick as possible with the next teaching element.

So let's take something like a basic sit - for it to be **reliable** and for your dog to actually respond in the important situations that you want them to, for example, when visitors come to the house, when meeting people out and about, when at the park, when you want to stop for a coffee at a cafe or a beer at the pub, there are around 15 levels of the training process, to achieve THAT degree of reliability.

Now, when you apply that same process to a 'problem' behaviour, something your dog has been doing that you don't want him to, for example your dog may pull on the lead, or be reactive, or not come back when called. In this situation, not only do you have to go through all the progressive levels of situational training, but you have also got to UNDO the established behaviour.

So please don't beat yourself up, or blame your dog, remember you're both learning, and as you can see, it's very easy to miss bits of the teaching process, meaning your dog might not always respond the way you expect them to.

To give you an idea....
If you have a dog that's 2 years old who pulls on the lead.
And you've walked your dog twice a day for their whole life

Your dog has practised the behaviour of pulling on the lead
(and been rewarded for it, from their point of view)
Around 1292 TIMES!

Imagine how good you would be at something if you practised it 1292 times.
Imagine how hard it would be for you to stop doing that, and start doing something different.
Can you see how this loops back to those habits we spoke about?

Does that make sense? Does that give you a better idea of why your teaching could only be working some of the time, and how much focus it takes from you to practise as much as your particular dog needs, because they're all different and what works for one may not for another. So remember what may seem like a small victory, is usually a HUGE step forward in the right direction, so make sure you give yourself and your dog a big (virtual) pat on the back! (or a glass of wine, not for your dog of course!)

So obviously I want to help you simplify all this, I don't want to leave you feeling like you're going to be trying to teach your dog for 5 hours a day for the next 2 years! So I have another Action Worksheet for you in the Appendix section at the end of the book, that I hope will help put it all into perspective and break down the process for you.

So, my question for you to consider is this...

If you have something you've been working on with your dog, but they're not as reliable at it as you would like, or when you really need them to be, ask yourself, and be honest now... Have you practised enough?

Essential Element #5
How to Make Teaching Your Dog as Easy as Possible!

I don't know about you, but I often have those weeks where things come up, you're sooo busy. Kids, jobs, spouses, family and all sorts of day to day problems are demanding your time and attention, and let's face it, it's all too easy for our dogs and their education to slip further down our 'To Do' lists.

Does that sound familiar?

Don't worry, you'll get no judgement from me, I know and appreciate exactly how this happens, it's called life, and it gets pretty distracting at times, which actually leads me quite nicely into Essential Element #5.

The problem is, from our Dog's Point of View, learning is taking place constantly, they're always watching and making associations, reading signals and learning to respond in certain ways to get things they want, or avoid things they don't want. So whether we like it or not, we're teaching them all day every day, and I don't know about you, but if my dog is going to be learning all the time, I would prefer to have at least some level of influence over what they're learning!

Teaching & learning happens all the time.
If you're not consciously teaching your dog,
They may be learning things you don't want them to.

So, how do we get around this? When life gets hectic and busy and lots of things take us off on tangents, things that need to be dealt with, does that mean we have no time to do any teaching with our dogs?

Well hopefully not if I can help you, despite all life's distractions, your dogs education doesn't have to take a back seat until you have time to 'get round to it', because the best, quickest and easiest way to make sure you can keep on top of your dogs teaching, is to integrate it into daily life, and make it fun and rewarding, much the same way we do with our children.

Which funnily enough loops back round to those pesky habits again, see how they all interlink?

You see, my habits are such that, I'm teaching my dogs most of the time, without even thinking about it. Again consider how you teach your children, throughout the day you teach them to always say please, that they must hold your hand to cross the street, that they must wait their turn to climb the slide and so on. Do my dogs feel like they're being constantly 'trained' ... nope! (well I hope not) because it's part of our daily life and it gets them things they want. I'm not commanding or ordering them around, it's the way our relationship is, and I make sure it's rewarding for them. My payback of course is that I get well balanced, well behaved dogs. ☺

They get to have lots of tasty things to eat, they get to do lots of wonderful fun things they want to do, they get more freedom because I trust them, and I get a reliably well behaved and responsive dog... all during the course of our everyday interactions.

Now if that's not a win win I don't know what is!

When you integrate your dogs education (training) into everyday life, it provides a LOT of opportunities for repetitions, which is the quickest way to strengthen and automate behaviours. It doesn't matter if it's general teaching you're working on, or trying to solve a problem behaviour, it still works equally well.

There are of course occasions when you do have to set aside time for specific teaching sessions. Like when you're teaching your dog something new for the first time. These initial learning sessions are normally at home and very short, 3-5 minutes max so very easy to fit into advert breaks, waiting for the kettle to boil etc. Usually within a few sessions, you're ready to take things on the road, whether that be at home or out on walks, and integrate into day to day life.

The other occasion when you may need to set aside time for specific learning experiences, is if you're dealing with an emotionally based issue. These can take longer to work through, and often require that you're able to work with your dog in controlled set up environments, whereby you can manipulate the situations and experiences, to make sure your dog is always comfortable and able to learn and progress without being pushed out of their comfort zones.

Aside from those two occasions, most other teaching activities can be integrated into daily life around the home and on your walks. I have made a list here, to give you some ideas of how easily you can integrate general teaching into your daily activities, to help you get started.

Examples of Integrating Teaching into Everyday Life

This list is not all encompassing, I've included some of the most common behaviours and in what situations, but hopefully it will give you enough of the general idea that you can take a look at your own dog, the things you're working on, and how you can integrate them into your particular lifestyles.

Behaviour - Sit or Down
Maybe these seem like basic unimportant behaviour's, but don't underestimate how useful a proofed sit behaviour can be, and practise makes perfect!

- ✓ Sit / down for their dinner
- ✓ Sit to go outside / Sit to come back inside
- ✓ Sit / Down to play tug or have a ball thrown
- ✓ Sit at every curb to cross the street
- ✓ Sit before jumping in the car / before jumping out of the car
- ✓ Sit before saying Hi to someone (human or dog) - No Sit, Don't get to say Hi ☺

Behaviour - Let's Go!
- ✓ Practise Let's go when your dog is sniffing on a walk and you're ready to move on (after you have let them have a sniff of course)
- ✓ Practise Let's go when you want your dog to follow you to get their dinner
- ✓ Change direction on a walk, and give your 'let's go' cue, then repeat to go back the original way
- ✓ Practise Let's go if you see dogs in the distance and you want to move away from them

Behaviour - Come Here (Recall)

- ✓ Practise recall around the home when you're about to give your dog a chew/treat/Kong
- ✓ Practise recall around the home between family members (Fun Game!!)
- ✓ Practise recall when you call your dog in from the garden
- ✓ Practise recall before you let your dog off lead (being let off lead can be the reward)
- ✓ Practise recall before releasing your dog to go play with another dog

Behaviour - Wait

- ✓ Ask your dog to wait before going out the door
- ✓ Ask your dog to wait while you lock the front door
- ✓ Ask your dog to wait at curbs before they cross the street
- ✓ Ask your dog to wait on walks, then release to go play
- ✓ Ask your dog to wait before bends in pathways on walks
- ✓ Ask your dog to wait while you pick up poo

This is a picture of me and Tramp playing a game of tug on a walk. Within this game we have integrated (played/trained) Sit, Wait, Get it, Drop it and Down, that's a lot of teaching, practise and fun within a very short time frame, and at a time when I'm out with my dogs anyway.

I hope that gives you an idea of how much and how often you can integrate teaching into everyday life. Although these types of exercises may not solve problems in and of themselves, they can all be highly beneficial to have as well practised and reliable behaviours, that can have a positive impact on other things. You will get a better idea of this in section 3, What to Teach and When.

Remember The Big Picture?

A problem behaviour is rarely a standalone issue, and the better engagement you have with your dog in all areas, the more fun you have interacting on a daily basis, the more likely you are to successfully work together in a partnership that makes achieving success seem a lot less challenging.

To Summarise the Essential Elements

1. Consistency is Key

2. Habits make it easier (Both yours and your dogs)

3. Check what the Big Picture looks like

4. Practise, Practise, Practise

5. Integrate into daily life and have fun

Things That Can Impact on Learning and Behaviour

I wanted to add a brief section here, just to make you aware that there are many things that can impact on your dogs behaviour, and their ability to learn and respond reliably. Sometimes, even when a dog does 'know' something very well and is usually excellent at responding to you, there can still be times when their responses might not be as reliable as normal. Here are some of the things that can have that effect, and some suggestions for what you can do to lessen the impact.

Remember, every dog is different, and some can be affected by things more than others, just like we can.

1. **Stress or Anxiety**
   Stress can affect a dogs ability to concentrate & learn, more on this in a moment. Be sure to address the underlying cause of the stressors. This may be achieved by creating distance, reducing pressure, breaking an exercise down into smaller chunks, managing either the environment, your dog or both.

2. **Bond, Trust, Relationship**
   As with any relationship a lack of connection can affect how well you interact with each other. Practise lots of engagement and focus exercises and take the time to learn how to listen and read all the ways your dog communicates with you using body language, facial expressions & vocalisations.

3. **Age**
Puppies, adolescents or older dogs can all learn & respond differently at times. Make sure your teaching set up is appropriate for the age of your dog. Have patience, understanding & an awareness of any other contributing factors listed here.

4. **Genetics**
Parentage, breeding, inherited character traits & genetic hardwiring can all have an effect on how well your dog learns, adapts, copes with & handles life in the human world. Know the typical character traits of your particular breed, take into consideration where your dog comes from & play to their strengths & natural abilities within their education.

5. **Past Experiences**
Because dogs learn by association & consequence, it doesn't take much for bad things to affect their behaviour, but equally good things can be promoted & strengthened to help overcome the effects of negative experiences. This is probably something you would benefit from professional assistance with.

6. **Level of Practise and Generalisation**
Unlike us, our dogs do not generalise well. If we want them to be able to do something in a variety of situations and circumstances, we need to help them generalise by practising in those situations & circumstances. This is covered in the step by step training guides.

7. **Character / Personality**
Some dogs are naturally more malleable than others, much the same as with humans. Take this into account when you're determining how you will motivate & reward them throughout their education.

8. **Your Behaviour**
Dogs are adept at reading us, our body language, our moods & our 'tells'. If things don't seem to be progressing, take a moment to consider how **your** behaviours may be influencing a situation before assuming your dog is being stubborn or not listening.

9. **Your Stress / Energy / Anxiety / Mindset / Focus**
Dogs first language is body language and energy. They know instantly when our moods change, when we're not focused, when we're stressed or anxious but they don't know why, so they just respond to what they feel. On a positive note, we can help them by consciously altering our behaviours and emotions to help influence theirs.

10. **The Weather**
Rain, cold, heat, fog and wind can all have an impact on how dogs feel and the look of the environment around them, which can subsequently affect their behaviour & responses. Wind can also carry smells a lot further, causing additional unseen distractions, especially to the hunting/scenting breeds.

11. **The Dynamics of a walk**
Who is on a walk can also change how a dog responds, both positively and negatively. If a dog is normally walked by one person, and then children join the walk, you could find your dog is more excitable and less responsive to requests. If you normally walk alone, but then

have a friend join you and you're distracted because you're chatting, you could find your dog being less connected than normal, or seems to have forgotten how to do some things they normally do well.

12. **Location**

Familiar locations can feel safer meaning your dog may be more inclined to travel further from you, OR that environment could be less interesting so they stick around more. New locations can be exciting, meaning your dog could be very distracted & easily disengage with you, OR they could feel insecure and uncertain, and therefore more likely to stick close by and look to you for confidence and reassurance.

13. **Distractions / Triggers**

Without the necessary practise in the presence of distractions our dogs can find it difficult to stay focused and respond. With situations involving triggers that cause our dogs to become fearful, anxious or reactive, it can make learning & responding very difficult for them. They need to learn in the absence of the triggers, and then be gradually exposed to them once they reach an appropriate level of confidence & ability.

14. **Health / Illness / Pain**

As with people, any illness or pain can have a profound effect on behaviour. If you're at all concerned, or simply unsure, get your dog checked by your Vet.

15. **Motivation / Rewards / Competing Environment**

How you will motivate your dog to make choices different to those they might make on their own, and how you will reward them for making those choices is a major part of successful teaching. Paying attention to the different levels of difficulty your dog may face when making those choices, and adjusting your teaching style accordingly is also important. There's more information for you on this key area, in the section coming up: How Will You Help Your Dog to Choose You.

16. **Distance**

Many dogs once a certain distance away from you can become detached and less likely to respond to your requests. Through daily teaching we can encourage our dogs to remain within a certain distance, thereby eliminating this disengagement.

Stress and Stress Stacking

Scientific studies in human physiology have proven that stress leads to health problems, makes us unbalanced, irritable, anxious or on edge, and it's the same for our dogs. Behaviours like aggression, destruction, excessive barking, over attachment and hyperactivity are all likely to have stress as a part of their root cause. Often these dogs are merely reacting to a situation in which they feel unable to cope or don't know how else to behave.

Many people recognise these as problems, but try to solve them by working on the problem behaviour itself, rather than taking into consideration any stress elements that could be **causing** the behaviour. So for a dog that barks excessively, yes you can work on teaching them to 'Shush' on cue, but if you don't resolve the emotion or cause that is driving the barking behaviour, your success is likely to be limited.

Spend some time watching your dog, paying close attention to the subtle signals they give about how they're feeling. If you think your dog's problem behaviour could be caused by stress, fear or anxiety, enlist the services of a force free professional to help you deal with the root cause of the problem.

By understanding how stress, good or bad, can impact our dogs behaviour, it enables us to make sure our responses are appropriate.

> ### From The DOG's Point of View:
> *Maybe you have a dog that reacts to other dogs when out walking, barking and lunging on the lead, and your response to this is to pull on the lead, shout at them 'No' or 'Be quiet', tell them off, maybe even smack them?*
>
> *The truth is, many dogs bark and react to other dogs when they're on a walk because they're anxious about the situation, it's a stress response to something they feel unable to cope with.*
>
> *Their two instinctive options when feeling threatened are fight or flight. If they're on a lead, they know they can't run away, therefore their only option is to fight, so they try to 'scare' the other dog off by barking at it, thus avoiding a fight.*
>
> *If your response to your dog's reactive outburst is to tell them off, from the Dog's point of view, not only are they anxious about the other dog, but now also anxious about your behaviour toward them, and will see the other dog as the cause of that. So this makes them even more anxious about the whole situation, which makes them want to make that other dog go away even more!*
>
> *The only way they know how to make the other dog go away, is to bark even MORE ferociously at it, so it doesn't come near them and make unpleasant things happen.*

So can you see how, by misunderstanding the driving emotions behind your dog's behaviour, **your** behaviour and emotional reactions could actually have a negative impact on them, instead of a positive one.

Acceptable levels of stress are present in a dog's life all the time, and are necessary to stimulate and encourage growth, but when these challenges become constant or unbearable, that's when stress can become a problem. Some dogs at this point can display growly, snappy or biting behaviours while others may shut down, seeming like they're okay, when in fact, it's possible they've become unable to deal with the situation at all.

As with humans, each dog will react to stress in different ways and at different levels. Something that may cause one dog to become stressed would not necessarily another. They each have their own baseline stress levels, and thresholds, which is the point at which they become overwhelmed and may react or shut down.

Many of these signs of stress are perfectly normal doggie behaviours, but what's important is the context. For example, if your dog scratches a lot on a walk, they could be feeling anxious.

Possible Signs of Stress

- Nervousness – easily startled
- Restlessness – unable to calm down
- Poor concentration
- Pulling on the lead / Biting the lead
- Refusal to take treats they would normally take at home
- Panting (especially if it's not hot)
- Lip Licking - especially when people or other dogs are approaching them
- Yawning (when not tired)
- Scratching
- Shaking (as if shaking off water)
- Destructive behaviours
- Excessive barking
- Over-eating or pica (eating inedible things)
- Loss of appetite
- Skin problems – Allergies

What Can Cause Your Dog to Become Stressed

Possible things that could elevate your dogs stress levels are many and varied, and as previously mentioned, are individual to each dog. Some may be obvious, but others not so much, here are a few examples:

- Changes in routine
- Shouting
- Being hugged and kissed
- Being stared at
- Pulling on the lead
- Pain
- Illness and/or medication (e.g. steroids)

- Boredom
- Aggressive handling or training
- Training classes in an enclosed space
- Confusion (Lack of consistency)
- Being left alone for too long, or too often
- An over stimulating environment
  - Parties in the home - especially children's
  - Large group training classes
  - Dog parks
  - Fetes, Country Fairs, Boot Fairs
  - Long days out in new places
- Any strange situation or new environment the dog is not familiar with
- Strange people the dog is not familiar with
- Strange objects
  - Umbrellas
  - Balloons
  - A new ornament
  - A dumped bag on the street
- Loud noises both in or outside the home - could include fireworks, sirens, workmen noise
- Travelling in the car
- Visiting the vets

An Explanation of Stress Stacking

Remember those days when everything seems to go wrong, you wake up late, the kids are playing up, you lose your car keys, the traffic is a nightmare, your boss is on your case, your hubby's in a bad mood and you manage to burn the dinner. Just as you're about to sit down and relax, you drop a glass and it smashes all over the floor and you burst into tears, or fly into a rage. The incident of the glass smashing wouldn't normally send you into a meltdown, but because it came after all those other things, your reaction was uncontrolled and out of character.

Well the same thing can happen to our dogs. There are two ways stress stacking can affect our dogs, it's not always about the negative things like vet visits or things that make them anxious, it can also be happy or excited stress, muck like when over excited children 'act up'.

Stress is stress, whether it's good stress or bad stress, too much of it can cause problems in behaviour. In the case of negative stress, the hormonal spike that occurs, can take up to 6 days to subside completely, meaning if your dog is constantly being placed in, or exposed to situations that cause them to become excessively anxious, concerned or afraid, their stress levels are never actually dropping completely. This can leave you with a dog that finds it difficult to relax, is always a bit on edge, may startle easily and be quick to react to things. So you can see how much this situation can impact on your dogs behaviour and ability to learn.

As previously mentioned all dogs have different stressors, and to varying degrees and stress stacking can play a part in that. Your dog is not able to manage their environment or many of the situations they find themselves in, so it's up to us as their guardians, to learn to read their signals and communications and manage their environment and experiences if necessary. In addition to this, we can help them learn how to be more comfortable in situations that distress them or cause over arousal through structured teaching exercises.

The Teaching and Learning Process

No matter what you're teaching your dog to do, or stop doing, the basic process is generally the same.

1. Try to get into the habit of saying your dog's name before asking them to do something, unless they're clearly engaged with you already. We talk an awful lot, so our dogs can switch off to most of the verbal chatter they hear from us. By saying their name before asking them to do something, they learn that what follows their name applies to them.

2. Learning should always take place in the least distracting environment possible, which is usually a quiet room at home. Imagine trying to learn a complicated dance routine, from a foreign speaking instructor, in front of an audience of 100's of people? How well do you think you'd be able to concentrate and understand them? But go home, practise that routine over and over, and before you know it, you can perform it with any level of distraction going on, because you already know how to do it. ☺

3. Teach & strengthen behaviours at home and in the garden before trying them out on walks. For example, if your dog can't walk on a loose lead in your garden, they probably won't be able to do it out on a stimulating & exciting walk.

4. Manage your dog whilst they're learning. For example, if you don't have a reliable recall trained, then your dog is not ready to be off lead yet, you need to prevent them running off **while** you teach them not to.

5. Have fun! We ALL learn better, faster and more deeply when the learning process is fun, and this is never more important than when teaching our dogs.

It may be 'training' to us, but if we do it right,
it's all just fun and games to them. ☺

Levels of Learning

1. Installing the Behaviour

The 1st stage of learning should always take place in a quiet location with no or very few distractions. A quiet room at home is usually ideal. Then when your dog understands what to do, you can drop in little practise sessions all over the house, sometimes quiet, sometimes busy with family or friends visiting.

2. Testing the Learning

Next stage is to practise in the garden, or just outside the front of your house, a little more distracting but still a very familiar place. If your dog can't respond to you in these places, then they're quite unlikely to be able to out in the real world, with all the sights sounds and smells to distract them.

3. Strengthening with Practise - Building Muscle Memory

Start practising in different low level distraction areas and on familiar walks. Quiet corners of fields, empty parks or even just walking up and down outside your house on the street. If your dog is struggling to concentrate, you could just keep going back & forth in the same area to make it more boring, rather than continuing to move forward to new ground all the time with new smells & distractions. Once you've had a couple of successful interactions, move on and try again in a little while, going back and forth again if necessary to regain attention.

4. Proofing - Making the behaviour reliable for when you really need it

Proofing a behaviour is the process by which you can help your dog learn to listen to you and respond to your requests no matter where you are, or what's going on around them.

You can achieve this by gradually starting to build up the level of distractions where you practise. Places like busy playing fields or parks, places where other dogs might be walking or playing, children's playgrounds, boot fairs, fetes, town centres, country fairs.

Remember though, if your dog is very distracted and finding it difficult to listen and concentrate when you first start practising in higher level distraction areas, see if there is a way you can create some distance from the distractions, or stay on the outskirts so you're able to move in and out as your dog acclimatises. Then once they can concentrate better, you can gradually move closer in small steps, taking care to notice stress levels and move back if necessary.

5. Add Duration (If required)

Gradually increase the amount of time your dog will remain in position if the behaviour requires it. Build up in small increments & always try to finish a training session before your dog gets bored, or fails to be able to keep their position.

NOTE: When you start to add Duration to a behaviour, you need to reduce distractions back to low level (or none) to start with, then add them back in again as your dog improves.

6. Add Distance (If required)

There are two ways you can add distance to your dogs behaviours. It may be that you want your dog to remain in a position while you move away from them. If this is something that you need, now you can start to gradually build up the distance you're able to move away. Remember to progress in small increments, don't go from moving 1 ft away straight to 20 ft away all in one go, take it one step at a time.

The second way you can add distance to your dogs behaviours, is if you need them to respond to you **from** a distance away, like if you need them to wait, or stop when they're 20, 30, 40 feet ahead of you. Now you can start building this into behaviours, again very gradually, building up a small distance at a time.

NOTE: When you start to add Distance to a behaviour, you need to reduce distractions back to low level (or none) to start with, then add them back in again as your dog improves.

Have Patience, remember how it feels to learn, especially when you don't speak the language. If things aren't going well, do something your dog finds easy and finish there.

Have You Heard of Positive Brain Focus?

All this means is: It's more effective to teach a dog what you WANT them to do, than to try and stop them doing something you DON'T want them to do.

Instead of trying to explain to your dog (which is very difficult because they don't speak our language) that you **don't want** them to do x, y or z, get it clear in your mind **what you want them to do** instead, and then focus on how you can communicate this to them. Help your dog to find a Yessssss!

When teaching our dogs, it's also better for **our** brains to focus on and create a positive thought process like '**stay by my side**' rather than a negative one like '**stop pulling**' which tends to create a feeling of resistance even just thinking about it. Did you feel it?

Try it now....
Think 'stop pulling' and see how those thoughts/words make you feel?
Now Think 'Walk close' or 'Walk with me' and see if that feels any different?

The second one just feels more inviting and engaging doesn't it? Even something as simple as this change in the way you think when you interact with your dog, can make a difference to how your dog feels, whether they pull on the lead or not, and how easy they will find it to learn.

How Will You Help Your Dog Choose You?

I've joked many times with clients saying 'I don't really know how to teach dogs, I just have the right food in my pocket.' ☺

Joking aside, whilst it's obviously not something that's going to miraculously turn your furry little Cujo into a model dog that wins every award for great behaviour, it's definitely something that's going to have a major impact on how easily your dog learns, how fast they learn and how much fun you both have doing it. Even without me teaching you anything, get this bit right and you could find yourself automatically making better progress with your dogs teaching exercises.

Important information for helping to get your dog to WANT to choose you:

✓ Short teaching bursts prevent boredom & stress and promote engagement & fun - which is why integration is the best way to teach.

✓ Manage your dogs behaviour if necessary whilst teaching, to help to guide them toward making the most rewarding choice and prevent them putting themselves in any danger.

✓ Punishment and harsh teaching methods damage your relationship and result in stress. A stressed dog is unable to learn, much the same as you would find it hard to learn if your teacher was being mean to you and you were stressed or anxious.

✓ Be aware how you use your voice - Commanding, shouting or angry tones can stress and confuse dogs and make it less likely they will respond to you. Nobody likes to be 'ordered' around, or shouted at, and our dogs are the same. You're teaching your friend, how would you like someone who was teaching you to talk to you?

Working out how you're going to motivate your dog to choose to do the things you want them to do, instead of all the things **they** want to do, and then how you will reward them for making that choice can be tricky with some dogs.

Do you know many people who would work a forty-hour week for a sack of potatoes?
Would a vegetarian work for a company that paid its employees with meat vouchers?

So why then do so many people expect their dogs to STOP doing all the fun stuff they want to do, and do the stuff us humans want them to do instead... for nothing?

It's not a bribe, it's a reward...
It's a 'Thank you'...
It's a 'Well done that was freakin awesome!'...
It's a 'you know what, you're great'...
It's a 'what a smart dog you are'...
It's an 'I LOVE what you did for me!'

Now tell me how many of you would NOT want to feel that on a daily basis? Well I know I would!

How many of you would not feel motivated to do MORE of whatever it was that got you that feeling? Which is what you want your dogs to feel right?

So, once again every dog is different and you have to determine what your dogs motivators are.

The first key points to consider are:

- What does your dog like? What is important to them?
- What does your dog love to get, have, or play with?
- They don't all like the same foods or toys
- Some like to be tickled, some don't,
- Some like to play, some don't.

It's important that you work out what ***your*** particular dog likes and doesn't like.

For most dogs food is very motivating (the right food) but for others it could be playing tug, catching a ball or having a game of chase with you. For some it might be things like life rewards, getting to play with other dogs, getting to go jump in the stream or rummage in those bushes. By finding out what motivates your dog and to what degree, it can help you control how much enthusiasm it's possible to create within your teaching exercises.

For my Border Collie Sky, it's all about the toys! Although she does love her food too, so we start with food rewards during the learning stages and then switch to toy rewards as we progress. This is because toys get her too excited which makes it hard for her to concentrate and learn, so you can see how these motivators are all important.

The better (higher value) rewards and motivators need to be saved for the harder exercises:

- Teaching new behaviours
- Working in high distraction locations
- Working to change emotionally based behavioural responses (for example reactivity)
- Requesting sharper, faster or more instantaneous responses

What Are You Competing Against?

Also consider from your Dog's point of view, what you're competing against. For example, if I were to take my Romanian Rescue dog Tramp on one of our familiar walks, and we were doing some impulse control exercises, which he can still struggle with from time to time, I would probably take something like chopped ham and hot dogs. These are things he likes quite a lot, but we do have them fairly often so they're not super special anymore. If however I was taking him to a local woods where I know there are a lot of squirrels, I would need to have more firepower in my pocket, something like cooked beef, liver or chicken, otherwise he is simply not going to disengage from those squirrels! He might the first time, but if my way of saying 'Fantastic that was an awesome choice!' is the equivalent of a limp handshake, next time he's just going to stay fixated on that very exciting and entertaining fluffy tailed creature.

The level of the reward must be relevant to the difficulty
of the choice being made by your dog

So you can see how, if you use the high value rewards for the easy stuff, you will have run out of firepower to make the choice worth it when things start to get challenging. It can also work well to use a variety of rewards, some high, some low, some medium; this can help maintain interest, because your dog never knows what you might pull out of the treat bag!

Treat Rewards

- Treat rewards should be quite small, about the size of your little fingernail to enable your dog to take the treat but not have to spend time actually eating it.

- Treats are best if they're soft and as healthy as possible because in the early stages you're going to be rewarding a lot, plus being soft reduces the risk of choking if your dog doesn't chew them properly.

- You need to consider how much food your dog is getting and lower their daily feed ration as appropriate. If you're carrying out a lot of teaching sessions and you don't adjust the daily food ration, your dog may gain unnecessary weight. (especially with Labs ☺)

I have added a list of possible motivators and rewards that you can experiment with for your own dog(s). By keeping a note of what are high and low motivators, you're able to alternate between rewards depending on the type, level and location of the exercises you're working on. This little thing, can make the difference between your training sessions being successful or your dog switching off in favour of something more interesting.

Treat/Reward Suggestions

The following reward suggestions and their level of worth / motivation are obviously based on my personal experience and so could be completely different for your dogs.

Low Level Rewards/Motivators

- Praise / Tickles
- Toys that your dog always has available
- Small treats your dog has regularly
- Their daily kibble / dog food

Medium Level Rewards/Motivators

- Excited Praise / Tickles
- Favourite Toys / Squeaky Toys
- Chopped Hot Dogs
- Chopped Sausages
- Meat or fish based commercial dog treats

High Level Rewards/Motivators

- Party praise / Crazy tickles
- Special Toys (only for playing with you or going on walks)
- Cooked Chicken/Turkey/Beef/Lamb
- Small thinly sliced squares of cheese
- Cheese Strings or tubes of cream cheese
- Chopped ham
- Chopped liver or heart (lightly cooked)
- Tuna cake / Liver cake
- Homemade treats using meat/salmon/tuna

For rescue dog Tramp, a bum scratch is actually around a medium level reward!

Create your own reward level table, so you can keep track of what you need when, depending on the exercises you're rehearsing with your dog. Remember, how you reward the good choices your dog makes, is the difference between rewarding them with £1 or £20. Low level is fine for the easy stuff, but when they look away from that distraction, or give you that first spot on response, you want to be dishing out those £20 notes to begin with, to make sure your dog knows this really is a choice worth making.

Low Level Rewards (£1.00)	Medium Level Rewards (£5.00)	High Level Rewards (£20.00)

Jackpot Rewards

There can be many occasions when giving your dog a jackpot reward is going to really hit home the message that what they did was perfect, helping to make sure it sticks in their mind, increasing the likelihood they will do it again next time!

Some examples might be when your dog gets something right for the first time, or when they disengage from something they find very distracting, or when they respond super quick or perhaps even when they don't do something you've been trying to stop, like jumping up or barking.

Jackpot rewards can be:

☺ A handful of treats given quickly one after the other as you heavily praise your dog for getting something super right!!

☺ If it's safe to do so, a handful of treats scattered in an excited, fun way, over a small area of the floor in front of your dog, as you heavily praise your dog for getting something super right! Just make sure there are no other dogs around that might try to swoop in and steal them or cause an argument over them.

☺ Something your dog finds highly rewarding in life. For some that could be a tug toy coming out of nowhere and a crazy game of tug. For others it might be getting released to go play off lead, or even things like being invited to jump all over you and have crazy time! ☺

But What If My Dog Won't Take Treats

Quite a common statement I hear from clients when I first meet them, is that their dog isn't food motivated or won't take treats when they're on their walks. Whilst it's true there are some dogs that aren't food motivated, over the last 15 years, I haven't met very many that were **truly** not food motivated in any way, after all its built into their survival mechanism. Usually there's an underlying reason and we were able to motivate them in other ways, which actually then led to an increased interest in the right kind of high level food treats.

So let's start with the most common reasons a dog won't take treats when out on walks, and what you can do about them.

Reason	Solution
Your dog is free fed & therefore may not be hungry	Feed your dog at set meal times and walk/teach before dinner time.
Your dog is overweight	Work to reduce your dogs weight and always walk / teach before dinner time.
Your dog has just been fed	Alter your daily schedule so your dogs walks take place before they're fed.
Your dog see's food treats as a bad thing (maybe you have bribed them to trim nails/bath them etc)	Try using high value real meat treats, not anything you have used before.

Your dog may be sick	If your dog usually takes treats but suddenly stops, get them checked by a Vet.
Your dog is over aroused	The underlying cause for each of these reasons will be different but the solution is similar. You first need to address the cause, lower the arousal/stress level, reduce environmental influences to lower stress/anxiety and at the same time use very high value real meat treats or maybe something like cheese if your dog is ok to have it.
Your dog is stressed	
Your dog is anxious	

Obviously this is a just a quick summary of reasons and solutions, if you do have a dog that doesn't take treats on walks, it would be worth working with a force free professional, at least to start with, so they could help you address the reasons behind it and enable you to move forward faster with your teaching.

Reducing Your Food Rewards

Another area of great confusion is when and how you reduce your food rewards as you progress through your dogs education, obviously most people don't want to be treating and rewarding forever. I have to admit though, I never leave home without something tasty in my pocket, because you just never know what might happen. It's far better to be prepared for a teaching opportunity should one arise, than have something fantastic happen, like your dog turns on a sixpence away from a deer or a rabbit, and all you have on offer to reward them with is a pat on the head and a well done mate!

That being said, when we're starting out on any teaching exercise with our dogs, the rate of treat rewards (if that's what you're using) is going to be higher, and it's that level of rewarding we don't want to be doing any longer than necessary.

One thing I do want to point out first though, is that there are no hard and fast rules with this, rates of reward can be fluid and interchangeable, every dog is different, and every circumstance is different. For example, I might be working on recall exercises with a dog, and they're doing great, so I may start reducing the treat rewards gradually. Then we might change location, so I would increase the rate of rewards to begin with, because of the change in the dynamics and distractions within the new environment, and then reduce them again once the dog is responding well again.

I would also increase the rate of reward when adding distractions to a previously learnt exercise. So if I had a dog that would happily walk nicely on a lead by my side in familiar places, I wouldn't be rewarding hardly at all, but if I took them to a very busy and stimulating location, an area with lots of off lead dogs or anything that may make them a little anxious, wildlife, farm animals or things like that, I would increase the rate of reward until they were able to relax and return to walking calmly on a loose lead again.

So the general rule of thumb is

- ✓ Start to reduce the rate of rewards you give as your dog gets better at the exercise you're practising. Do this gradually, so start to reward randomly, and keep an eye on how well your dog continues to do the exercise, so you can switch it up or down as necessary. I always give praise and tickles, even if I'm not rewarding with treats or toys.

- ✓ If you change location, it's likely you will need to increase the rate of reward again to start with, until your dog settles in that new environment.

- ✓ If you add distractions, it's likely you will need to increase the rate of reward to start with, until your dog settles and generalises to the new distractions.

- ✓ Switch your treat rewards to toy rewards if you have a dog that prefers toys. I usually recommend having separate special toys for when you're out on walks, that get put away once you get home. This keeps them interesting, special and prevents them being destroyed on a regular basis if you have a chewer!

SECTION 2
Step by Step Teaching Guides

All of The Dog's Point of View's EBooks, teaching guides and worksheets are based on teaching dogs using force free positive reinforcement methods. Successful outcomes, and having a well behaved dog, is largely dependent upon the foundation of a successful relationship where both dog and guardian are connected with each other. **Respect**, **trust** and **co-operation** are what makes a successful relationship possible.

Positive reinforcement methods enhance the relationship between you and your dog, ensuring you both have fun, which means your dog should learn faster, better and their education will be long lasting.

A lack of connection between dog and guardian
can be a significant obstruction to effective learning

Although it may seem like there is an awful lot of life skills shown here that you need to teach your dog, because every dog is different, every relationship is different and every lifestyle is different, you may not need them all. Some may be significantly useful to you, while others not so much. Some may be useful to you today, while others may become more beneficial to teach at a later date.

It is worth remembering though, if you're experiencing problems with your dog around the home or out on walks, the more situation appropriate behaviours your dog knows, the more 'right' behaviours they have to choose from, the less likely they are to make their own decisions about how to behave, which will be instinct based, meaning they will simply do whatever feels right to them as a dog. So jumping up, barking, lunging, growling, dragging you down the street or running off to chase anything that moves, are all very natural (and at times fun) dog behaviours that, in the absence of any previously taught more appropriate behaviours, your dog will automatically revert back to doing, because that's what comes naturally to them.

I have created a PDF File to accompany this book, which contains just the workbook elements for you, should you wish to have additional pages, or a separate set of worksheets and challenge lists in case you have multiple dogs in the household. Please feel free to contact me via the website at www.thedogspov.com if you would like a separate set of just the worksheet elements. I have also created a playlist in the The Dogs Point of View YouTube channel where video demonstrations of the exercises in this book will be uploaded.

Marker Method of Teaching

Most of the following step by step training guides are based on a marker method of teaching. In my experience this is a highly effective way to teach these exercises, and can really help dogs and their people learn to communicate more effectively. Most dogs LOVE learning this way.

You may have heard of, or even tried clicker training, which is a marker method of teaching. I use the term marker teaching because not everyone wants to use a clicker, so wherever you see the term mark/reward or mark/treat within the training guides, the marker can be whatever you choose.

- A clicker
- A marker word like 'Yesssss!' said in a light, snappy tone
- Making a clicky noise with your mouth
- Or something else

Whatever you choose to use as your marker, it needs to be consistent, which is why an actual clicker can be more effective. It's a very distinct sound that our dog's don't hear very often (unlike our voices!) and it's always the same. Having said that, there can be times when we don't have our clicker with us, so I must admit, I usually recommend to clients, even if they choose to use a clicker, to get into the habit of saying the 'Yessss!' word alongside every click, so if ever they don't have a clicker with them, they always have their marker word.

The way that marker training works is by teaching your dog, in the first instance, that your marker predicts a reward. This is very simple and an explanation of how to do it is coming up. Then you are able to use the marker to give your dog a clear notification that what they did at THAT moment was what you wanted, and it will be followed by a reward. Your reward, whether it's food, toys or play always **follows** the marker, it isn't given at the same time. So although it's ideal for it to be given as quickly as possible following the mark, it's not the end of the world if it takes a second or two on occasions, the click or marker is what lets your dog know they got it right. We all have that fumbling in the treat bag problem sometimes!

A common confusion around marker training, and clicker training in particular, is that you use the clicker to GET your dogs attention, this is not how it works. You can teach your dog to respond to a specific attention getting noise, or interrupter noise, but for the purposes of this explanation, marker (clicker) training is used to MARK wanted behaviours, so the mark has to happen at the same time the desired behaviour happens.

So the marker method of teaching is basically a communication tool that enables us to effectively explain to our dogs they did the right thing. As previously mentioned, dogs learn by association and consequence, so being able to provide this consistently timed feedback helps our dogs learn faster, with less confusion, less stress and makes it more fun for them. I mean, who doesn't like to hear the sound of 'Yep you win! A reward is on the way' Taking into account that dogs will do more of a behaviour that gets them something they want, you can see how this allows us to build and strengthen the behaviours we would like our dogs to do more of, and a natural consequence of that is seeing less of the behaviours we would rather they didn't do.

So if your marker sound pinpoints the moment your dog does the correct behaviour, as you can imagine the timing is very important. The delivery of your click or mark can mean the difference between your dog learning what you want them to, or something completely different! If this isn't anything you've ever tried before, I do recommend you practise your marker timing without your dog present to start with, that way you can learn and perfect your skill without having any negative impact on your dog. You can set yourself up for success with the following simple exercises.

Timing Exercise 1

1. You need a tennis ball and someone to help you.

2. Have your clicker with you, or know what marker word or sound you're going to use.

3. Have someone drop the tennis ball for you, and as it makes contact with the floor, you mark it with your click or marker sound.

4. Remember, if you think 'click' as the ball hits the surface, you will be too late. The average persons reaction time is 0.3 seconds, which may not sound much, but when you're working with your dog, it could mean the difference between teaching your dog a down, or a play bow, you would be surprised how perceptive and literal they can be!

Timing Exercise 2

1. You need a friend to help you and your clicker or marker word/sound.

2. Have your friend stand in front of you and slowly raise one of their arms outwards from by their side, in an arc up to their ear.

3. The point of the game is for you to click or mark the point that their arm is horizontal from their shoulder.

4. Now this should be fairly simple at the beginning, when they're moving their arm very slowly, but with each repetition ask them to move a bit quicker, and a bit quicker.

5. As you will see, once they start moving quickly, it becomes harder to 'click' them to stop in time, but practise makes perfect!

As you read through the following teaching guides, you will see me mentioning the 'CLICK Point' or 'MARK Point' and this is just my way of explaining to you, the exact moment you're aiming to click or say your marker word, in order to correctly mark the behaviour you're working on.

Charging the Marker (Clicker) - Pairing the Marker with the Reward

Before you can start using your clicker or marker effectively to communicate with your dog, you need to let your dog know that Click = Reward (or whatever marker you've chosen). This is super simple to do.

If you want to use an actual clicker, and your dog is hearing the clicker sound for the very first time, stay a little way away from them or put the clicker behind your back until you see how your dog feels about the noise. Some dogs can be noise sensitive and some clickers are louder than others.

1. Simply grab your clicker/marker and a tub or treat bag full of tasty treats your dog loves.

2. Be somewhere with no distractions at a time your dog is calm but not sleepy.

3. Click your clicker or make your marker sound and immediately give your dog a treat.

4. You don't need to ask your dog to do anything, don't say their name, simply mark and treat.

5. Repeat for 10 treats.

6. Take a short break and repeat again for another 10 clicks/marks + treats.

7. Now you can test the association.

8. In a different room to where you've been pairing your marker, have some treats hidden in a pocket out of sight and wait for your dog to look away, then make your marker sound and see if they look at you.

9. If they instantly whip round, ready to receive that treat, then you know they have made the association that the marker = reward (remember to give them their treat!)

10. If they don't look or react in any way to the noise, continue to repeat the exercise above, and re-test the association again in a different room after a couple more sessions.

11. Once you know your dog has paired your marker with the reward, you're good to go!

Important Rules of Marker/Clicker Teaching Method

✓ You only click or make your marker noise once.

✓ Your marker noise or click must always be followed by a reward, which is why it's better to have a distinct marker sound. If you don't maintain this, your marker could lose its value - As your dog gets better at each exercise and the need to reward becomes less frequent, get into the habit of praising 'Good boy/girl' instead of marking, that way you don't need to reward/treat every time.

✓ The reward always follows the click or mark, never present the reward before the click.

✓ Make sure you don't reach for the reward before you click - your smarty pants dog will pick up on this!

Practise your LEAD TECHNIQUES

Well practised lead techniques are an essential part of many exercises

- ✓ Loose Lead Walking
- ✓ Impulse Control
- ✓ Reactivity
- ✓ Engagement

Why is Our Handling of the Lead So Important?

One of the most important aspects of being able to maintain a great connection and level of engagement between you and your dog on walks, is being able to release tension in the lead when necessary. It's also going to be more pleasant for both of you if there's minimal straining or jerking on the lead from either end, even by accident.

If you're pulling against your dogs pulling, or even holding onto them as they strain against the end of the lead, because dogs have opposition reflex, they're going to find it very difficult to stop leaning against **you**. It has to be you that learns to break the cycle.

Opposition Reflex: All this means is, whenever our dogs feel pressure against their bodies, in this case their necks or chests, they will automatically lean against it, humans do it too. If I were to push against you, you would push back against me to prevent yourself from being pushed over.

This is what happens with your dog, if you're pulling or holding tightly **against** their pulling, they will continue to pull against your pulling... Goodness, did you follow that?! ☺

The following techniques, once practised, should help you learn how to quickly break that pulling cycle, and learn how to use the lead as a communication tool instead of a controlling one.

Practise being able to SLOW STOP

Practise the technique of slow stop so that as soon as your dog gets a step or two in front of you, you're able to bring them to a standstill without yanking, jerking or pulling them. This means you both remain relaxed, rather than creating tension and frustration, and from here you can regain their attention and reposition them by your side, or ask them for another behaviour.

As soon as your dog is a step or two in front of you

1. Place your free hand further down the lead gently to help stabilise yourself.

2. Stop walking and balance yourself. I find this best by having my feet in a stride position and keeping the arm holding the lead in a right angle position, so it's locked but not tense.

3. Bend your knees slightly, lean in toward the lead as you apply gentle pressure, whilst at the same time allowing your forward hand to slide back towards you along the lead, bringing your dog to a slow stop.

This may take a little bit of practise, so don't worry if you don't get it right straight away. It will come!

LEAD WALKING

This is a really handy technique that enables you to get closer to your dog, but without pulling on them and creating more tension in the lead. For example, you're walking along a track with your dog relaxed at the end of their lead or long line, and your dog alerts to something, maybe another dog or a small furry animal. Although they haven't reacted yet, you know they might do and need to be closer to them to ensure they can't launch themselves forward, and to give you greater control over manoeuvring them if necessary. If you just pull on the lead to get them back to you, you increase the risk of causing a reaction and you create tension in the lead that is likely to cause them to pull harder against you.

1. Let's say you have the handle of the lead in your left hand, as your dog alerts to something immediately place your right hand onto the lead, a bit further along from where you're holding the handle.

2. Keeping hold of the handle, place your left hand further along in front of your right hand, so you're walking hand over hand down the lead.

3. Repeat this hand over hand action, folding up the lead with each hand as you go, until you're right next to your dog with them on a nice short manageable length lead but without tension, so although the lead is now short, make sure you're not pulling.

4. You're now in a position to regain their attention and either simply connect with them as you both watch the distraction go by or move away, or you can give them further instruction to 'Let's go' or move 'Over' or 'Sit'. The likelihood of them being able to respond to your instruction has increased, because you're now close beside them, and they know that you're also aware of the distraction.

LEAD RELEASE

If your dog has a tendency to stand hanging on the end of the lead, lead release is a simple technique to relieve the tension in the lead, which in turn should help your dog to soften their body against the lead at the other end.

The technique for lead release is very simple

1. With one hand holding the handle of the lead, place your other hand further down (this is your stabilising hand)

2. Gently open and close your stabilising hand on the lead, in a soft squeezing motion.

3. This not only helps to relieve the constant tension in the lead, but also in your arm and hand, helping to break the pulling cycle you're both stuck in.

4. Be watching your dog and you should see (and feel) them visibly soften against the lead.

5. As soon as this happens, release your stabilising hand so you're just holding the handle of the lead again and it loops loosely between you and your dog.

6. You can then regain their attention, reposition them or ask them for another behaviour.

LEAD STROKING

Lead stroking is a calming technique from the TTouch method of working with dogs. The technique for lead stroking is pretty much what it says on the tin. If lead release doesn't work, you can easily switch to lead stroking as an alternative.

1. As your dog stands leaning at the end of the lead.

2. One hand will be on the handle of the lead, and place your other further along the lead and begin gently but firmly sliding this hand back and forth along the lead.

3. This transmit softness down the lead, and creates a gentle vibration which helps release the tension of the pulling cycle for you both.

4. As you do this, you should see and feel your dog begin to calm and the tension reduce (less pulling)

5. When this happens, relax the hand holding the handle of the lead (but keep hold of the handle) and use this hand to stroke the lead as well, in a hand over hand type movement, taking each hand forward and stroking back toward you along the lead.

6. Your dog should have stopped pulling against you at this point because you've released all the tension in the lead, giving them nothing to pull against. You can now regain their attention, reposition or move away depending on the situation you're in and where you need to go next.

Teach your Dog HAND SIGNALS

Why teach Hand Signals

- ✓ Dogs read body language more than listen to vocal cues
- ✓ Builds stronger engagement
- ✓ Your dog will usually check in more often when taught using visual signals
- ✓ It looks pretty cool when your dog responds to hand signals only!

Personally, I like to add hand signals to everything I teach whenever and wherever possible. At the end of the day, a dogs first language is body language, and although they may not always be looking at us when we're out on walks, if we've laid the right foundations within our relationship and teaching exercises, there should hopefully be a high degree of visual interaction between us. This is one of the main purposes of teaching a Conditioned Name Response that is so reliable, it works no matter what our dogs are doing or what distractions are around. We need them to look when we call their name, so we can then give further instructions, whether they be verbal or a visual hand signal.

In an article written for Psychology Today by world renowned Scientist, Professor of Psychology and Author of numerous best selling and award winning canine books, Stanley Coren, he quotes a study that shows dogs respond to visual signals with 99% accuracy, and verbal instruction with 82% accuracy. Furthermore within the same study, when these dogs, who had already been taught to respond reliably to both verbal and visual cues, were given conflicting verbal and visual signals, for example, verbally asked to sit whilst being given a hand signal to lay down, the dogs responded 70% of the time to the hand signal over the verbal request.

Teaching your dog hand signals - step by step

1. PLEASE NOTE: It's important to teach your dog using a **verbal** cue word **first.**

2. Choose the hand signal you want to pair with each behaviour.

3. Give your hand signal first, closely followed by the verbal word your dog already knows.

4. At this stage your dog is responding to the verbal word.

5. Repeat for 10-15 treats giving your hand signal just before your verbal word.

6. Take a break and repeat for another 10-15 treats.

7. Test your dog's response by giving just the hand signal, if they respond, give them a jackpot reward! If they don't respond instantly, wait a few seconds to give them a chance to figure it out for themselves, but if they don't respond within about 10 seconds, they probably haven't got it yet, so give the verbal cue word.

8. Continue to practise giving the hand signal slightly before the verbal word and re-test again after another couple of sessions.

9. Only work on teaching one hand signal exercise at a time until your dog is responding instantly to that one.

10. Teach a hand signal for each behaviour individually.

Teaching a CONDITIONED NAME RESPONSE
(Or in English - Play the Name Game)

Why teach a Conditioned Name Response

- ✓ If you cannot get your dogs attention in any environment, you have nothing to work with.

- ✓ Let's your dog know what follows applies to them

- ✓ Enables you to get your dogs attention whenever you need it, to manoeuvre them, give further instruction or interrupt unwanted engagement to the environment

These exercises may seem simple and unimportant but they're the foundation upon which all your other exercises are built. If you can maintain attention from your dog **under any circumstances,** then you will be able to give them information about what you want or need them to do next.

If, however, when you say your dog's name, you get nothing... If you can't even get them to look at you, you've got nothing to work with! You could tell them you have prime rib steak and a bitch on heat in your pocket and it won't mean a bean, they're not listening.

Now I know most of you will probably say 'Well of course my dog knows his/her name', and of course they do, but do they answer you EVERY time, even when there are all manner of distractions present will they turn and look at you in response to their name.

Imagine you live in a house full of Russian people, and you don't understand Russian. So most of what these people say, you begin to zone out, because you have no idea what it means, and it doesn't seem to be relevant to you anyway. Quite often throughout the day, you hear your name, so you look, but nothing happens, they don't want anything from you, or show any indication they're talking to you, or that you're to do something. So eventually, you stop responding to your name most of the time. Then, suddenly you become aware they're repeating the same word over and over, increasing in volume, and when you look, they're manically indicating to you that they want you to do something, but you had no idea they were talking to you, because they didn't say your name?

Can you imagine how this might relate to your dog?

We often say their names when we don't actually want them for anything, and we often ask them to do things without saying their names first, especially when we're out on walk, or we JUST say their name, without adding anything instructional afterwards, to give them a clue as to what we actually want them to do.

Bottom line, if you can't get your dogs attention when you're out on a walk, whenever you need it, you may struggle to ask them to do anything else, be it call them back, ask them to disengage from something, get them to stop or simply follow you in a different direction.

So here is my advice for you:

1. Take some time to make sure you teach your dog that whenever you say their name, you need them to respond (technical term - teach a conditioned name response)

2. Get into the habit of using your dog's name before you ask them to do something, so they know that amongst all the other gobbledy gook (another technical term!) that comes out of our mouths - when they hear that word (their name) it means whatever comes next applies to them.

3. Become aware of how much you use your dog's name when you don't actually want them for anything.

Set Yourself Up for Success

✓ Make sure you're in a quiet area with nothing else going on to start with, you want to be certain when you say your dog's name, they will look.

✓ Do not ask for any other behaviour, don't ask them to sit or come to you, all your dog has to do is **respond** to their name.

✓ The click/Yessss! will tell them a reward is on its way.

✓ If you have multiple dogs in the household, work this exercise with them separately.

- ✓ If your dog is responding really well and you feel they can move onto the next step, then go ahead, but if they start to fail at any point, you may have progressed too quickly, so go back to the last stage they were responding reliably.

- ✓ Progress steadily, especially if you have quite a high degree of disconnection with your dog on walks. Don't start expecting your dog to respond to their name in highly distracting environments until you've conditioned this response at the earlier levels.

Teaching a Conditioned Name Response - Step by Step (The Name Game)

1. Starting at home, have some tasty treats in tubs around the house, and as you go about your day, randomly say your dog's name in a happy tone, just once and give them a treat. They don't have to do **anything**, not even look at you at this point.

2. After 10-20 repetitions of this, you should find, because home is very familiar and doesn't have many distractions, they will start to look at you, as soon as you say their name, if they weren't already.

3. NOW you can start letting them know that THAT is exactly what you want!

4. The second they look at you, THAT is your 'CLICK POINT' (or 'Yessss!' point)

5. Give them a couple of treats as you praise them and then continue what you were doing.

6. Once you've practised at random times over the period of a day at home, you can start taking the game outside into the garden, which will be more distracting.

7. When you let your dog out into the garden any time, after a short while, go out, say their name, MARK it & treat them (as long as they look of course)

8. If you're close to them, you can give them the treat, if they're a little way away from you, you could gently throw them the treat, adding fun to the experience as they snuffle for their reward.

9. Wander away from them and leave them to get distracted again, then say their name again.

10. Repeat this a few times, then go indoors.

11. IMPORTANT: Don't keep repeating their name, say it only once (This is quite difficult if you already have the habit of repeating things when you don't get a response, but stick with it, wait a second or two to see if they respond, practise makes perfect)

12. If they don't look, you may not have set the situation up to be easy enough for them at this new level. See Possible Problem below for solutions.

13. ***Possible problem:*** If your dog doesn't respond to their name in the garden

    a. The environment may be too distracting this early on in the game - have your dog on a lead to start with, then progress to off lead when they get better at the game.

    b. Move closer to your dog - make sure you give 2 or 3 treats if they do look.

    c. Use higher value treats.

    d. Go back to playing the game indoors for a bit longer and make sure they're responding really well there before trying in the garden again.

    e. Make sure they don't need to go to the toilet.

14. Once they can play the game in the garden, you can nip out whenever they're out there and have a quick practise, giving you several mini sessions throughout the day.

15. Once your dog is responding really well at home & in the garden, this should only take a couple of days, it's time to take it on the road!

16. Start randomly saying your dog's name when you're on your daily walks. Don't do it too often though, so it gets boring and nagging, and when you first start doing it, try to pick times when you're almost certain they will look, times when they're relaxed and not busy doing something. Your dog won't learn anything by repeatedly failing.

17. Work progressively through the following challenges for The Name Game, ticking them off the list as you practise and your dog gets really good at each one ☺

(NB: Really good means your dog will look at you when you say their name 80-90% of the time... there is no such thing as 100% when dealing with dogs!)

List of Challenges for Conditioned Name Response

Challenge: Can Your Dog Respond to their name...	Yep! My Dog Can Do That
In every room of the house	
In your Garden at home	
When stood outside your house, about to go for a walk	
As you walk along the street outside your house on a normal lead (or somewhere equally familiar & fairly quiet)	

Challenge: Can Your Dog Respond to their name...	Yep! My Dog Can Do That
As you walk along any street on a normal lead (NOT when your dog is sniffing)	
When on a field/countryside walk on a long line	
When your dog is sniffing something *NB: Sniffing is really engaging for dogs, so the first time they respond to their name, whilst they're busy sniffing, make sure you give them a JACKPOT reward*	
When on a field/countryside walk with your dog off lead (if allowed) but close to you *NB: If your dog likes to catch treats, you could gently throw the treat to enhance the fun of the game*	
When on a field/countryside walk with your dog off lead 20-30ft away	

Challenge List for Strengthening & Proofing the Name Response Behaviour

With the following challenges, if any of these things are triggers for your dog, i.e. they find them incredibly distracting or can be reactive toward them, you will need to make sure you're at a distance from them that your dog is comfortable with and so can remain relaxed, otherwise the exercise will fail, and that doesn't help your dog learn and progress.

Challenge: Can Your Dog Respond to their name...	Yep! My Dog Can Do That
When they're on lead and have alerted to another person or dog	
When they're on lead and have alerted to anything that interests them (a cyclist, child on a scooter, football game, children playing etc)	
When they're on a lead or long line and have alerted to countryside creatures (Squirrels, pheasants, ducks, geese, deer etc)	

When they're off lead, quite close to you and have alerted to:
  ✓ People
  ✓ Dogs
  ✓ Children
  ✓ Cyclists
  ✓ Countryside Creatures
NB: When you get to testing at this level, you need to be fairly certain your dog is going to respond before trying this off lead, we don't want them ignoring you and running off to self reward!	

With any trigger situations, once your dog can respond at their comfort distance, then you can start to try at closer distances if the opportunity arises during your walks, but always be aware of your dogs stress and arousal levels, so you can manoeuvre them away to a more comfortable distance if necessary. This is not about putting pressure on them to respond, it's about setting them up to succeed, that is where the powerful learning takes place.

Possible Problems

✓ ***Your dog doesn't seem to understand***
If at any point as you progress through these challenges, you fail to get a response from your dog 3 times in a row.

- You have possibly progressed too fast, go back to a level your dog can do well at and continue there for a bit longer to strengthen the behaviour before progressing.

- You have possibly increased the levels of distraction too quickly, go back to less distracting situations.

- Move closer (if appropriate)

- Ensure your motivation is appropriate for the stage you're at - Use higher value treats.

- Ensure your motivation is appropriate for the level of distraction you're working with - Use higher value treats.

- Have your dog on a lead or long line to prevent complete disengagement from you.

- Your dog may be stressed, tired, needs to go to the toilet or is simply not in the mood for the exercise you're doing. Try something different or end there and let your dog tell you if they want to continue.

✓ ***It's ok to help them out in the beginning***
You may just a few times, give your dog a clue, such as the ones shown below to get them to look at you, but you don't want to keep giving them clues, or they won't learn the behaviour for themselves and it will never be strong when you need it.

- Make a sudden movement, mark/treat.

- Make a little kissy / hissing noise that causes them to look, mark/treat.

✓ *Your dog just keeps staring at you & following you around*

- Use lower value treats & have them in your pocket not in view.

- Disengage from your dog, wander off, go and do something else until you see them become disinterested, then you can say their name again.

Note: This is not a constant exercise, obviously we want you and your dog to relax and enjoy your walks, and we certainly don't want them to get fed up with the sound of their name! So you're aiming to drop this game into your walks randomly but not constantly, and practise it using the progression of challenges in order to proof the behaviour, so they automatically respond when you need them to.

By now you should be getting regular, reliable responses from your dog at a variety of distances, in different locations with any number of distractions around them. As long as you're getting a high level of responses from your dog in all these locations, you're well on the way to having a dog with a conditioned Instant Name Response behaviour!! **Congratulations**!

Teaching A VOLUNTARY CHECK IN

Why Teach a Voluntary Check In Behaviour

- ✓ Establishes an unspoken communication system
- ✓ Encourages engagement when on walks
- ✓ Strengthens the bond between you and your dog
- ✓ Allows you to give your dog more freedom knowing they will check in and not just go ahead and make their own decisions

This is hands down one of the easiest and most effective ways to build engagement with your dog out on walks, and by their choice! (Eventually ☺) What's even better is, that it's never too late to teach and strengthen this behaviour and develop your position as your dogs guardian and therefore the person best equipped to make the important decisions in the relationship.

Many of our dogs can get themselves into trouble when they make their own decisions about what they do on walks. Running off to see people or other dogs, chasing things, getting themselves lost, these are all behaviours that are quite normal for dogs, but nonetheless ones that can be dangerous for them.

By practising and strengthening this behaviour, you should be able to enjoy more freedom with your dog, feel less stressed about situations like having them off lead (if they have a reliable recall trained of course, which this exercise will help with) and feel more connected with them. By really engaging and enjoying the time you spend together, rather than just wandering along in your own world, and they in theirs, they remain aware of where you are in proximity to them the whole time.

Teaching Voluntary Check In - Step by Step

1. You can start this exercise at home, with just 10-15 treats at a time, and as you move around the house, each time you catch your dog looking at you, THAT'S your CLICK POINT (or Yesss! point) instantly mark that look and reward them with a treat.

2. We're not asking for anything so no cue word is used for this exercise, don't say your dog's name or anything, just 'capture' when they look at you, this is a choice we want our dogs to make purely on their own.

3. After a day or so, start taking this exercise outside, start on lead, somewhere not too distracting, and simply mark & reward every time your dog chooses to look your way.

4. Initially, because you're now outside with all the distracting sights, sounds and smells, your dog most likely won't check in with you to start with. You may need to be a little creative in getting those first few check ins, to help your dog understand that the same game applies no matter where you are.

5. You could try slowing down, stopping, shuffling your feet, sniffing or making a quiet kissy noise. These are all good ways to elicit a quick look back, which you can then mark, reward and carry on.

6. That's it! That's all you want from them for this exercise, to get into the habit of regularly checking in with you by choice.

7. If your dog has a reliable recall and is allowed off lead in safe places, you can practise voluntary check in and reward them by tossing the treat. For some dogs this really enhances the pleasure of the game, as they can either have fun catching the treat or enjoy snuffling in the grass to find it, a very enjoyable and natural behaviour for your dog.

You can find some video's on The Dog's Point of View YouTube channel, of my rescue dog Tramp doing some early stages of Voluntary Check in on a long line, you can see how I am slowing down slightly to elicit the look back. Then a second video a week later of Tramp doing Voluntary Check in off lead, choosing to remain engaged with me, even when he gets slightly distracted.

Kicking it Up a Notch - Check in With Distractions

Once your dog has got the hang of this game out on walks in low distraction areas, you want to start strengthening the behaviour so your dog will look to you for instruction whenever they see something.

The most important part of this section of learning, is that your dog is managed and under control, so they can't make a wrong choice. This enables you to create the ideal circumstances for them to learn the 'check in' game and win!

So this stage requires that you actively seek out all sorts of different distractions. I wouldn't recommend starting with something you know is going to send your dog into 'hyper dog land', so for example, if you know your dog gets seriously over excited when they see another dog, leave that one until further down the list. You can of course still practise the exercise if you need it, if you come across another dog, but try and keep your distance, this will give your dog every chance of actually being able to disengage and look back at you.

You could make a list of things your dog finds distracting and then order them from lowest to highest level of distraction. If your dog can't look away from something at the lower level of the distraction list and be able to check in with you, they won't be able to with things at the higher end of the list. By working through your list from lowest to highest, you're progressively building and strengthening the behaviour of voluntary check in, meaning it will become more reliable in everyday life.

Distraction List Example
Your list will of course be specific to your dog as an individual, but it may include some of the following:

Example List	Your List
Strange looking objects	
People	
Children playing	
Cyclists/scooters	
Birds	
Squirrels/Rabbits/Cats	
Other Dogs	

The teaching process for this is simple

1. With your dog on a lead or long line, locate a distraction they will show interest in.

2. Keep enough distance so that your dog doesn't get over excited.

3. When your dog notices the distraction you bring them to a slow stop, saying nothing.

4. Wait for them to look away from the distraction and back at you.

5. Mark it (Clicker or Yessss!) and reward with food treats or toy (maybe a tug game?)

6. If appropriate, move forward a little further and repeat the exercise again if your dog looks back at the distraction. Stop and wait for them to check in, mark it, reward then move on.

7. If the distraction is something your dog is allowed to have or do, like perhaps it's a dog you know and they're allowed to play with, you could use going to play with the other dog as a **wonderfully powerful** reward for the check in. Be sure to give your dog a permission word though, something like 'Ok Go See' or 'Go Play' so they know it's ok, otherwise they may learn to check in, but then run off thinking they're automatically allowed! ☺

8. If the distraction is something your dog isn't allowed to have or do, then once they have checked in, continue to move on past the distraction (with a 'Let's go' or a 'This Way') repeating the exercise as necessary. At some point your dog should **stop** looking at the distraction completely, at this point give them 4-5 treats one after the other with lots of praise as you both walk away together.

9. ***Possible Problem:*** If your dog is very distracted and struggling to disengage

   a. Give them a clue - shuffle your feet, make a kissy noise, move into their eye line.

   b. Be sure to give them a jackpot reward when they do, and move away from the distraction in a fun, excited way to boost the reward for them checking in with you.

   c. **Remember:** You haven't **asked** them to do anything, so even though they may take a long time to make the right choice, they still made it in the end and we want to make sure they know 100% that what they did was fantastic, even though they found it hard to do.

   d. Make sure you set your dog up to succeed by choosing distractions they will be able to disengage from, or at a distance from a distraction they will find easier.

Challenge List for Voluntary Check In

Start with lowest distractions first, and leave out anything that is a trigger for your dog or causes them to react. This is a great foundation exercise to have in place for trigger situations, but there are some other foundation exercises you will need to do before your dog would be able to voluntarily disengage from a trigger. Add your own challenges to this list, relative to where you walk and your dogs distractions and remember to have your dog on a lead or long line if necessary.

Challenge: Can Your Dog Disengage & Check in...	Yep! My Dog Can Do That
When they see a strange object	
When they see people on a walk	
When they see other dogs on a walk	
When they notice a bird or squirrel	
When they alert to cyclists or children on skates or scooters	
Add your own challenges...	

Points to remember

- ✓ Once your dog understands the game, continue to practise on your walks, the more you reward for this behaviour, the more often it will get offered.

- ✓ You have to seek out any particular distractions you want to practise with, but remember to start at a distance.

- ✓ If you're going to reward your dog with being released to go and see the distraction once they have checked in with you, make sure you teach & use a release word, so if it's not ok sometimes, they won't assume it's ok to check in and then go anyway.

- ✓ If your dog is very distracted by something, THEN checks in with you, make sure to give them a Jackpot Reward!

Once your dog is doing this really well, you can start to practise with them off lead if it's safe to do so, or with a trailing training line for added security and management in the early stages. Just be confident your dog is within reach and isn't going to run off with the training line attached.

Teaching a VOLUNTARY CLOSE

Why Teach a Voluntary Close

- ✓ A very effective exercise for teaching your dog to pay attention to you, again by choice.

- ✓ An **excellent foundation exercise** for Loose Lead Walking

- ✓ A great exercise to use for when your dog is off lead but you need them to stay with you for a short moment

- ✓ An excellent technique to build natural connection into your relationship.

Teaching Voluntary Close - Step by Step

An important part of this exercise is that you say very little to start with, preferably nothing to your dog. The whole point of the exercise, is for your dog to work out for themselves what you want them to do, that way the learning that takes place is self educated, making it longer lasting and more reliable.

1. Start with your dog off lead in a very low distraction & **secure** environment

    a. your garden is ideal.

b. or a very quiet area of a field or park (although this is usually too distracting for them to concentrate enough in the early stages of learning) if necessary keep your dog on a long line to prevent them wandering off.

2. Have some very yummy, smelly treats in your pocket and give your dog one before you start.

3. Start walking away in a straight line, **say nothing**, if they follow you, when they reach your side THAT'S your CLICK POINT (Yesss! Point) At this stage, it doesn't matter which side, you can raise the bar later on if you want to encourage a particular side for this.

4. ***Possible Problem:*** If your dog doesn't follow you, but wanders off around the garden sniffing

   a. Make sure you have treats that your dog likes – very yummy ones!

   b. Pat your leg and move away sideways the first few times, to give them a clue.

   c. Hold the treat out so they can see it for the first few times only.

   d. Make sure your dog doesn't need to go to the toilet.

5. Immediately following your mark/treat, change direction and walk away again (to the right / left / about turn)

6. Again **say nothing** simply move off in this new direction (give a little clue if necessary). If they follow you, when they reach your side again, MARK & treat and give lots of praise.

7. You may need to manoeuvre yourself into helpful positions to start with until your dog gets the idea of the game, especially if you're trying to encourage them to walk on a specific side of you.

8. Repeat this in 2-3 minute sessions, be sure to stop before your dog gets bored.

9. Repeat several times a day, to help your dog learn quicker.

10. Once your dog is good at the game and is reliably keeping with you, begin to put a cue word to the behaviour ('close' or 'with me')

    a. Give your cue word immediately before you mark/treat, so as your dog arrives by your side, you say 'Close' then Mark & Treat. At this stage we're not asking our dogs to do the behaviour, we're still teaching it. So what you're doing here is associating the verbal word with the behaviour, and for that to happen correctly the word has to be said AS your dog is doing the thing you want. Using the cue word to GET your dog to come and walk nicely by your side comes later, once they've learnt the behaviour.

11. Once your dog can do this well in the garden, you can start to drop in little practise sessions when you're out on walks, for example a corner of a large quiet field or local park. *TIP: Have them on a long line to prevent them wandering away or if there's any danger of them running off.*

12. *Possible Problem :* If they begin to fail at this when you start to practise outside the garden.

   a. Find a place to practise that is less distracting, somewhere you walk all the time that is quite familiar and doesn't have a lot of new smells / distractions.

   b. Make sure you have high level treats.

   c. Go back to giving them clues for the first session or two (hold out treat/pat leg)

   d. Make sure your dog does not need to go to the toilet.

Integrating & Strengthening the Behaviour

Once you can see your dog is clearly getting good at this game, start practising it randomly on your daily walks, especially if you let your dog off lead. By doing this it not only develops and strengthens the behaviour, but is also periodically reconnecting you with your dog. It provides you with that all important opportunity for a fun engagement activity that helps to prevent them zoning out completely, which can result in them not listening to you when you do ask them to do something, plus it looks pretty cool to all the other dog walkers!

List of Challenges to Practise your Voluntary Close

Voluntary Close Challenge Exercises	Yep! My Dog Can Do That
Occasionally call your dog back, when there are no distractions and ask them for 'close' as you walk along. Release them to go play again	
Call them back and ask for 'close' as you approach a blind bend, to keep them safe. Release them to go play again	
Call them back and ask for 'close' if you see another walker, so they're with you ready to go back on the lead if necessary. Release to go play again	

With the next list of challenges, have your dog on a lead or a long line if necessary, to make it easier for them to make a great choice. If any of these challenges are triggers for your dog, avoid practising this exercise until you've completed the necessary foundation work for reactive dogs.

Practise your Voluntary Close Exercises	Yep! My Dog Can Do That
As you walk past another person out walking	
As you walk past children playing	
As you walk past another dog	
As you walk past other dogs playing	
As you walk past a cyclist	
As you walk past children playing with a ball/frisbee	
As you walk past a horse rider	
Add your own challenges...	

LOOSE LEAD WALKING - Foundation Exercises

Two of the exercises included in the step by step teaching guides are also excellent foundation exercises for teaching your dog to walk nicely on a loose lead.

These two exercises are:
- ✓ Voluntary Close (With me)
- ✓ Impulse Control

You can also use the following foundation exercises to really develop, strengthen and embed your dogs loose lead walking skills. For me personally, this doesn't look anything like a formal heel position, my dogs don't need to be pinned to my side looking up at me, they just need to be walking near my side with the lead loose between us.

Begin at the Beginning - Desensitise Excessive Excitement at Walk Times
Use the following steps to establish calm behaviour at home when getting ready to go for a walk.

- ✓ Desensitise your dog to all aspects of getting ready to go for a walk; this in itself will begin to help eliminate pulling on the lead because stress begins to accumulate from the moment your dog starts to get over excited.

- ✓ **Your behaviour** must indicate that nothing proceeds unless your dog exhibits calm behaviour throughout the process of getting ready to go for a walk.

- ✓ Repeat the desensitisation exercises as often as possible.

- ✓ Praise & reward your dog (calmly) for **all non excitable behaviour.**

- ✓ Ignore everything else.

What you're aiming for:

- ☺ Your dog to remain calm while you get ready to go for a walk

- ☺ Your dog to sit quietly while you attach their lead

- ☺ Your dog to walk calmly with you out of the house and begin their walk in a relaxed state

Sample Desensitisation Plan

	Your Behaviour =	A: Dog gets Excited =	B: Dog Remains Calm =
1.	Go to the cupboard and take out the lead	• Put the lead back • Repeat exercise later	• Praise calmly/quietly • Go to step 2
2.	Go to the cupboard and take out your shoes	• Put the shoes back • Repeat exercise later	• Praise calmly/quietly • Go to step 3
3.	Put your shoes on	• Take your shoes off • Repeat exercise later	• Praise calmly/quietly • Go to step 4
4.	Attempt to clip the lead on your dog	• Stop at once • Stand up & wait for calm • If they calm down, try again • If not put the lead away • Repeat exercise later	• Praise • Go for a walk!

Take it 1 Step at a Time

This technique is a PROACTIVE TEACHING approach, whereby our aim is to interrupt our dogs **before** they pull, so we can mark & reward the behaviour we want, instead of constantly trying to work backwards after our dogs have already pulled in front.

This is going to work best if you can practise in the garden first quite a few times, together with Voluntary Close, before starting to practise it on your walks out in the real world. This helps both you and your dog get the hang of the technique, away from all the distractions you face once outside in the streets and fields.

Imagine trying to teach a child their times tables whilst you're stood next to a playground full of children. As you would expect, they would find it hard to concentrate and therefore retain and remember the information. Now, take the child somewhere quieter and less distracting and teach them their times tables. Once they have practised and repeated them over a short period, you would be able to take them back to the playground full of children, and they would be able to recite their times tables, because they had already learned, and retained the information before you added the distractions to the experience.

1. Start with your dog on whatever side is most comfortable for you - it can be helpful to pick one side and stick with it, especially during the learning stages as this can provide more consistency for your dog to latch on to.

2. Make sure you have your treats in the pocket or a treat bag on the same side as your dog.

3. Take ONE step, as your dog steps with you THAT is your CLICK POINT mark and treat (if you're not using a clicker this is your Yessss! point**)**

4. Your aim is to mark or click before your dog takes a step ahead of you, which as you can imagine is likely to be easier in your garden than outside on a walk at this point.

5. Take another step, mark it/treat.

6. Continue to mark & reward as your dog steps with you.

7. Remember to smile and keep your body soft and light, especially the hand holding the lead, so you're attracting your dog to stay close to you (part of the engagement process)

8. If your dog gets ahead, bring them to a slow stop (see lead techniques) saying nothing.

9. It's important that you say nothing and try to let your dog work out for themselves how to make you get going again.

10. Wait a moment to see if they will check back with you to see why you've stopped.

11. If they do, instantly smile, say 'Hi' and use your body language to invite them back to your side.

a. Turn sideways

b. Bend forward slightly at the hips

c. Smile

d. Hold your left palm out (if you walk your dog on your left) down by your knee - as though you're inviting your dog to come and stand next to you.

12. As SOON as they arrive, smoothly begin to take a step forward again, which they should take with you, and THAT is your CLICK POINT, AS you're MOVING FORWARD, not when they arrive back by your side. Mark & treat them on the move only after at least one step has been taken - the treat delivery needs to be quite rapid at this stage to keep your dog where you want them to be and prevent them shooting straight out in front again. This rapid treat delivery is your constant feedback (communication) that THAT's the behaviour you want from them. (Don't worry this rapid treat delivery stage doesn't last long)

13. **_Possible Problem:_** If your dog doesn't check back in when you stop, but instead stands at the end of the lead looking around.

a. If there is tension in the lead, do lead release/lead stroking to elicit relaxation & a look back.

b. If the lead is soft, but your dog is still standing looking away from you, you could shuffle your feet or make a soft kissy noise with your mouth to get their attention, then as they look back, instantly smile, say 'hi' and invite them back so you can continue step/reward.

14. If you don't have a garden and need to practise this on your street outside your house, keep your walk to the same small area to start with, so you're not constantly moving into new sights/sounds / smells which are distracting and make it harder for your dog to concentrate. Once they've got the hang of the lead work in the same familiar place, then you can start expanding the distances you walk, but in the **learning stage**, they will pick it up quicker if they're covering the same boring ground and able to concentrate more on you than what's around them.

15. Remember to capture (with a Yessss! /treat) any moment that your dog looks up at you voluntarily.

16. Ensure this exercise is reliable in a low level distraction area before taking it into different locations with higher distractions.

17. ***Possible Problem :*** If your dog continually lunges forward

    a. Do more practise with Voluntary Close & Impulse Control Exercises before going on walks.

    b. Practise more in less distracting environments (home or garden, outside your house)

    c. Use higher value treats.

If your dog wants to sniff, then of course allow them to, this helps your dog relax and acclimatise to their surroundings. Sniffing is also a naturally calming & mentally stimulating behaviour which helps tire your dog out, BUT prevent your dog from pulling you to sniff something.

1. If they try to pull you to sniff something - bring them to a slow stop.

2. When they check back in with you to see why you've stopped, You can say, 'thank you, go sniff' and release them to go sniff the spot.

3. The 'go sniff' is a life reward so no treat reward is required for this.

Build & Strengthen the New Behaviour

1. Gradually start to increase the number of steps you take between each Mark and treat.

2. Remember though, you may need to go back to rapidly treating at the beginning of each new walk for a short while, then as your dog settles on their walk, you can start treating less again.

3. Practise this training in new locations - each time you change location, you may find your dog starts to pull again, because the change of location is new and exciting. So be prepared to go back a stage or two, but because your dog already knows the process, they should progress much quicker each time.

4. Once your dog will walk for quite a distance without a mark and treat, begin to phase out the marker.

5. Continue to praise and randomly treat your dog for a while longer, to establish the behaviour as their new habit.

6. Once the new behaviour of walking nicely on the lead by your side is well established, you can begin to phase out the food treats.

7. ***Possible Problem*** : If your dog begins to pull again

    a. You may be allowing them to pull on the lead sometimes?

b. You may have reduced the food treats too quickly?

c. Go back to treating (and if necessary Marking / treating) for a while longer.

d. Ensure the behaviour is firmly established before reducing the treats.

8. Gradually increase the level of distractions your dog has to deal with whilst continuing to walk nicely on their lead.

Add a VISUAL CUE

With body language being a dogs first language, it can be helpful to some dogs, when teaching them how to walk nicely on a lead, to provide them with a visual focal point (a hand position) to clearly communicate that at that moment, you need them to be walking calmly next to you. This can be an especially helpful tool to use for dogs that might be anxious about going for walks or can get over aroused (both of which can show itself as strong lead pulling behaviour)

As previously mentioned in the 1 step at a time exercise, your dog is going to be on a particular side, and your treat rewards are going to be delivered by that hand. The easiest hand signal to give your dog would be to hold that arm at a right angle with your palm up (once learnt it works equally well no matter what side your dog is on or what hand you use).

To begin with, you could have a treat in it, but as your dog can't see what is or isn't in your hand, I would only usually do this 3 or 4 times and then it would just be my empty upturned hand. If you find your dog begins to constantly have their head turned, staring beggingly at your upturned hand, or they begin jumping & grabbing at your hand (this can happen with serious foodie dogs) then you can just turn your hand over and show them it's empty, that should eliminate the behaviour within a few repetitions.

Obviously as you walk along, you're going to be marking and then reaching for your treat to give to your dog, so they normally learn quite quickly that the treat does not actually live in the hand, but comes after your mark.

I've found having this focal point for some dogs works really well during the learning stages, but I also use it quite a lot when my own dogs are off lead. I can ask them to wait if they're ahead of me, and although I may not need to put them back on lead, for whatever reason I want them to remain walking next to me, so I give the 'Close' (Voluntary close) hand signal, which helps to communicate to them with my body language and not just my voice, that for the moment, until released, I need them to remain walking along by my side.

Quickly and Steady

I like to teach my dogs the words quickly, meaning we need to get a move on (and sometimes THEY need to get a move on!) and steady, meaning slow down. These can be useful in any number of situations, both when they're on lead and off lead, and can be helpful to teach as part of the foundation exercises to help our dogs learn to walk nicely on their leads.

The more instructions we can give our dogs, to explain what we want, the less they're left trying to figure it out for themselves.

NOTE: Working on this exercise will probably be easier for both you and your dog if you've worked on both Voluntary Close and the 1 Step at a time exercise above prior to this one.

1. Start off at home in your garden or just outside your house on a very familiar street, just going back and forth over the same spot to make it easy for your dog to remain engaged with you.

2. Have a pocketful of tasty treats and your dog on their normal lead, give your dog a treat and then set off walking very slowly.

3. As they step with you THAT is your MARKER POINT saying your verbal word 'steady' as you give your dog their treat.

4. Continue to step very slowly, marking and saying 'steady' as you treat, praising them calmly and keeping their attention on you as you keep them moving steadily with you.

5. After about 10-15 treats of doing steady, start to speed up, if you have your dog well engaged they should automatically speed up with you, THAT is your MARKER POINT, treat and give your verbal cue 'Quickly' at the same time, in a nice upbeat tone to match your energetic walking.

6. Again continue to mark and treat giving your 'Quickly' cue word as you both walk quickly along together.

7. After about 10-15 treats of going quickly, start to slow down, saying 'Steady' in your calm voice.

8. Once again if your dog has remained engaged with you, they should automatically start to slow down with you, mark, treat and praise.

9. At this point take a break and let your dog go sniff! This is hard work for doggies!

10. You can do another round of steady, quickly, steady after a 5-10 minute sniffy break, or you can end there have a little game and practise again later in the day.

11. Once your dog can do this well in your garden or just on the familiar street outside your house, you can start saying the cue word first, get the response, THEN MARK & treat.

12. You can also start dropping it in randomly on walks, just for 2-3 minutes at a time which will help your dog to generalise and get really good at it.

If your dog has a good recall, or you're in a safe place, you can practise it off lead too, ending each session with a game of fetch or tug to reward your dog for concentrating and working so well with you.

Once your dog knows this exercise well, you can use it to help control speed when they're off lead, if you need them to come quickly, or if they're getting too far ahead of you, ask them to 'Steady' and slow down and wait for you to catch up.

Teach a General Wait Behaviour

When I'm working on loose lead walking exercises, I also build in teaching my dogs a general 'Wait' behaviour. It's not a formal stay, it is simply something I use as part of our everyday walks and it communicates to them I want them to wait until released to move. They don't have to be doing anything in particular, they can be sitting, standing or laying down, wait just means remain stationary until released. My release word is simply 'Ok Let's go' which of course ties in with my 'Let's go' exercise which means, I am now moving, come with me.

Teaching Wait - Step by Step

1. With your dog on a normal length lead, tasty treats in your pocket/treat bag.

2. As you walk along together, take a treat and slow to a stop AS you put the treat in front of your dogs nose & give the cue 'wait'. Your dog should easily stop with you and THAT is your MARK POINT , give your dog the treat.

3. Stand in that position for a few seconds, calmly repeating the cue word 'wait' treating each time you repeat the word.

4. Give your release word as you move off and praise.

5. After two or three sessions of this exercise, stop using the treat lure (having the treat in your hand) but still put your hand down in front of their nose and ask for the 'wait' at the same time as you slow down (This can then become your visual hand signal for wait). As your dog stops with you MARK and treat, hold the wait by repeating the cue & treating, release & move off.

6. Repeat often in lots of different scenarios, making some 'Waits' longer than others.

7. This is a great exercise to use on street walks at every curb. Sometimes I might ask for a 'Sit' after the wait, but mostly it's just wait and then release with 'Ok Lets Go' as we cross the street, again I will vary the length of time we wait.

8. Once your dog is really good at this, start reducing the treats, so I may repeat the cue word 'Wait' but not treat every time, gradually reducing them until I don't really treat at all, unless the behaviour starts to fade for any reason.

Additional recommendations for teaching your dog to walk nicely on a lead

✓ Have separate loose lead teaching walks & relaxing walks - If you don't feel like doing loose lead teaching then go on a relaxing walk instead, with your dog on a long line if they don't have a good recall.

✓ Drive to your relaxing walks so you don't have to do loose lead walking exercises to get there.

✓ Set a time limit for your teaching walks and stick to it, rather than try to get round a route. So whatever distance you get to at the halfway point, turn round and come back. It could take you a long time to get round a route in the early stages, and if things aren't going well, you could both end up getting very frustrated, and that is something that will definitely not help either of you.

✓ Keep teaching walks quite short around 15-20 minutes max, it's hard work for you both, and allow your dog to sniff if they want to, but no pulling.

✓ Everyone who walks your dog must be consistent and do the lead exercises or any progress made will be undone.

Teaching 'THIS WAY'

Why Teach 'This Way'

- ✓ A really fun game to play with your dog that can help prevent 'deafness'
- ✓ Can help prevent your dog from wandering too far ahead of you when off lead
- ✓ Can be used as a pre-cursor to recall training
- ✓ Can be useful as a distance gaining strategy for reactive dogs
- ✓ Allows you to give your dog more freedom knowing they're more likely to respond

'This way' can be a really useful behaviour to have in your toolkit when out and about on walks with your dog off lead. The way it's taught makes this a really fun game that most dogs love, so it sticks in their mind, often becoming really reliable with quick responses.

I actually use this more than Recall for keeping my dogs near to me on off lead walks, and of course to make sure they know which way I'm going!

Teaching This Way - Step by Step

Practise in one location to start with. For example in a small park or in a large area of field that doesn't have too many distractions. This is to strengthen the behaviour and your dog's response to it when they realise what a fun game it is! Once you've completed 5 or 6 sessions of teaching your dog how to play the 'This Way' game, you can start dropping it in randomly on your daily walks.

1. If your dog doesn't have a good recall, have them on a decent length lead (at least 6ft) or a long training line and harness, but keep the length of your long line limited so your dog can't get over excited and take off. This would risk them reaching the end of it at speed, and put you in danger of a yank to your arm and to their body if you're trying to hold on to them.

2. Have some soft, tasty treats with you that your dog really likes, and you want them to be a bit bigger than pea sized for this exercise, to make it easier for your dog to find them. Cheese works really well for this game, if your dog doesn't have any issue with eating small amounts of cheese of course.

3. As you walk along, turn and start to walk the opposite way, saying '<Fido> This way' in a light happy tone.

4. As your dog turns to come with you, start to trot/jog forward away from them and AS they catch up with you, THAT is your MARK POINT .

5. AT THE SAME TIME as you click (or mark) gently toss your tasty treat onto the grass just in front of you, not too far at this stage so they can clearly see it and don't charge off after it.

6. Once your dog has found the treat, walk a bit further in that direction then repeat the exercise going back the other way.

7. Repeat 4 or 5 times, then continue on walking /sniffing for a little way.

8. Randomly play the 'This Way' game throughout your walk.

9. As you and your dog start to get good at this game, you can speed up your jog away from them, making it into a 'chase me' game, encouraging them to come faster with your excited voice as you toss their smelly treat a little further away from you, so they then have to use their noses to have a snuffle and find it.

10. You could drop this game into a 30 minute walk at least 3 or 4 times, along with the Voluntary Check In and Find It games to improve and increase engagement.

11. Once you're getting great responses for 'This Way' on your walks, you can progress to playing the game when your dog is off lead, as long as it's safe to do so and your dog has a reliable recall behaviour, which this should help with. Start off in areas with little or no distractions to set your dog up to win!

Strengthening & Proofing 'This Way!'

Now your dog is good at 'This Way!' you want to start practising it with gradually increasing distractions, so it will be reliable when you really need it to be, no matter what is going on around you. Take care when you start using real life distractions on your walks, have your dog on a long line to begin with, to set them up for success. Also make sure that you run in a direction with space, and you're not going to run directly into another distraction.

You can also start to give your dog the treat reward sometimes at this point, instead of throwing it out in front if it could be a problem in the area you're playing (for example if there are quite a lot of off lead dogs around, best not to be throwing tasty food about) but remember to play the game now and again without distractions so your dog can enjoy chasing that thrown treat, they really seem to love it.

Your 'This Way' Challenge List

Can Your Dog do a 'This Way'...	Yep! My Dog Can Do That
When you see people walking ahead	
When you see children playing nearby	
When there is another dog in the distance	
When there are other dogs playing ahead	
When you see a cyclist	
When you see horses coming	
Add your own challenges...	

Testing Your Engagement - The Bungee Game

1. Ensure you're in a safe environment & there is no risk of your dog running off, have them on a trailing long line if necessary, and maybe a helper with you in case they don't play the game!

2. Start playing this game WITHOUT giving the 'This Way' Cue. This encourages your dog to naturally and automatically keep an eye on where you are, because you have become unpredictable.

3. Let your dog get a little ahead of you, then just turn around and go the other way, keeping an eye on them to make sure they've noticed you're moving away from them. As soon as they realise, and come running after you, lots of praise & have a jackpot treat party!

4. Repeat, Repeat, Repeat going in different directions then finish and continue on your walk. Drop it in again later on to build the voluntary engagement.

5. If your dog notices you're moving away, but doesn't come after you, they're probably not ready for this level of the exercise yet or maybe you've tried it in an area that is too distracting. Try practising in a less distracting environment.

Teaching a PROOFED SIT

Why teach a Proofed Sit Behaviour

- ✓ Sit is one of the easiest things to teach our dogs, and it's usually a very comfortable position for them

- ✓ Sit is often a better option than down to anchor your dog, many dogs can feel vulnerable being made to lay down in situations they feel unsure about

- ✓ Your dog can be taught to sit when at a distance from you quite easily

- ✓ Sit can be easily integrated into daily life, making it an excellent default behaviour choice for our dogs

- ✓ Sit encourages calm and engagement

Teaching a Basic Sit Behaviour (If you're dog doesn't already have one)

1. Using a medium value treat, put it on the end of your dogs nose and slowly move it backwards and upwards slightly.

2. Your dog should follow your lure and if you hold it in place, moving with them if they move backwards, most dogs will drop their bottom down quite quickly.

3. The moment your dog's bum touches the floor, THAT is your CLICK POINT and give them the tasty treat.

4. Repeat a few times, then do the same hand movement but without the actual treat in your hand, as their bum plops down, mark and reward as before from your pocket or a nearby tub of treats.

5. Repeat without the treat lure a few more times, then start to add your verbal 'Sit' word - you want to say the word AS your dog's bum hits the floor, not before at this stage, we are pairing the word with the behaviour.

6. Once this is going really well, you can start giving your 'Sit' request to your dog along with your hand signal (which at this point is still your hand pretending to hold a treat near their nose) while they're standing, and they should respond with a sit, mark, praise, reward!

7. Practise over a couple of days, gradually moving your hand away from their nose, deciding on what hand signal you want to give for sit. The most favoured are raising your hand, or a finger pointing up, but it can be any hand signal you choose as long as you're consistent with it, and everyone uses the same.

Start with Sit for Everything

Once your dog is sitting reliably every time you ask them, you can now start to incorporate sit for everything into daily life. Using a hand signal & verbal word to start with, sit for everything is like the 'Please' of the doggie world. We want our dogs to figure out that Sit gets them a lot of great stuff, which means this is likely to become their 'Go To' behaviour, instead of all the other sorts of things they try when they want our attention or want to do something.

1. Start incorporating your sit request into daily life.

    a. Sit for dinner

    b. Sit for treats

    c. Sit to go out in the garden

    d. Sit before having their lead clipped on

    e. Sit before going out for a walk

    f. Sit for a fuss/tickle

    g. Sit for a ball to be thrown

    h. Sit before grabbing the tuggy toy

i.   Sit to say hello to people

j.   Sit to cross all roads

k.   See if your dog can Sit randomly throughout his daily walks - this builds up the strength of his default 'Sit' behaviour even when there are lots of distractions.

2. To begin with ask for the Sit with your voice/hand signal but after a couple of days, start to say nothing and just wait to see if your dog offers a sit (an automated sit behaviour) this will show they're learning and embedding the behaviour well. For example just wait...

  a.   As you hold the lead ready to clip on, say nothing and see if they offer a sit.

  b.   As you wait at the front door to go for a walk, say nothing and see if they offer a sit.

  c.   As you hold a treat in your hand, say nothing and see if they offer a sit.

  d.   As you hold the ball ready to throw it, say nothing and see if they offer a sit.

  e.   When your dog offers that sit, mark it **& praise massively, instantly rewarding** them with whatever the activity was, so it's clear to them that 'Sit' was what you wanted.

3. Make sure you give your dog a chance to figure out what you're waiting for, but if they aren't offering a sit within about 10 - 15 seconds, it may be you've progressed a bit fast. So ask for it again with your voice/hand signal and then try again later or the next day without the verbal or visual cue's and see if they can work it out.

Proofing Your Sit so It's Reaaaally Reliable!

Once your dog is sitting well, it's time to strengthen the behaviour so it's really reliable, you can ask them to sit anytime, anywhere and they will remain calmly sitting by your side, even when there are lots of distractions around them. At this stage, you also need to teach a release cue, so your dog knows clearly when it's ok to move on.

Why is this important?

Our dogs don't understand much about our human world or the environments and situations they find themselves in, and they make decisions based on their experiences and how they feel. This is often what happens when they behave inappropriately and cause problems, or worse put themselves (and maybe you as well) in danger. By being able to clearly ask them to do something very easy, that will make them stationary and calm, we're able to prevent all manner of problems cropping up.

So your dog is now sitting really well for many things and getting lots of great stuff for it. This is the time to add challenges and pay them heavily for being able to stay sitting. This is how you PROOF your sit behaviour.

I don't usually expect my dogs to remain sitting and watching me constantly during these exercises, but I do like them to check in periodically and so will pay them for that too when practising.

Personally I don't teach a formal 'stay' behaviour, I don't really do anything with my dogs that requires it, but they do know that 'wait' means whatever you're doing, stay where you are. So they could be standing or sitting or laying down, and I will use 'Wait' to prevent them from moving until released. You could teach and use a formal 'Stay' instead if it suits you better.

Work through the following list of challenges with your dog to get the most amazing default Sit behaviour!

List of Challenges for an Awesome Proofed Sit

As always, if any of these challenges are triggers for your dog, make sure you're at a distance from them that your dog is comfortable with and so can remain relaxed, otherwise the exercise will fail, and that doesn't help your dog learn anything. Also, to begin with, don't ask them to sit for too long each time, build this up gradually over time using your stay (or wait) request.

Challenge: Can Your Dog Remaining Sitting...	Yep! My Dog Can Do That
When someone walks into a room in your house	
When someone offers them a treat in your house	
When someone calls them from another room (you can release to go find)	

Challenge: Can Your Dog Remaining Sitting...	Yep! My Dog Can Do That
To have their lead clipped on	
At the door before leaving for a walk	
At the curb to cross the road	
When people are passing by	
When people with dogs are passing by	
When children are playing nearby	
When a cyclist goes past	
When a jogger runs past	
When other dogs are nearby playing	
Add your own challenges...	

Teaching IMPULSE CONTROL

Why teach your dogs to have impulse control

- ✓ Helps your dog to develop self control around distractions & in arousing situations
- ✓ Can be effective in maintaining focus & engagement with your dog on walks
- ✓ Can be an excellent pre-cursor training tool for Loose Lead Walking.
- ✓ An important part of your dogs general basic education

Many of a dogs natural behaviours are kind of inappropriate for our human world and lifestyles, but we don't want to kill their spirit completely, or remove all their fun. We really want to be able to give our dogs as much freedom as possible, but at the same time we need to keep them safe, and teach them how to make good choices by themselves without our constant intervention, this is where teaching impulse control becomes invaluable.

By developing a certain set of 'default' behaviours through learning, repetition and consistency, we are providing our dogs with a clear communication of things they need to do in particular situations, even though they may prefer to do something else.

Teaching Basic Impulse Control - Step by Step
(Based on the It's Yer Choice game by Susan Garrett)

1. Choose an appropriate level food reward for this exercise. If your dog is very food motivated, use a lower level food, if your dog is not then use a higher value reward to make sure they're interested.

2. Hold a small handful of the food in your enclosed fist, 10 or 12 treats, and hold it a short distance from your dogs nose.

3. They will most likely push/nibble/lick etc to try to get the food, that's ok, say nothing, just leave them to keep trying. At some point they will stop and look away or back away.

4. When they stop trying to get the treats OPEN your hand, BUT be ready to close it quickly again if your dog tries to dive in and grab those treats, which they most likely will to start with. Still saying nothing.

5. No words are necessary, your actions as a consequence of your dogs behaviour are all the communication your dog needs. Just let them work out for themselves what they need to do, they will learn faster that way.

6. Repeat this open hand/close hand until your dog will stop going for the treats when your hand is open. THEN you can MARK IT and take a treat from your hand and give it to them.

7. Do not allow them to help themselves from your open hand.

8. If they stay where they are and don't attempt to go for the treats, you can mark & feed again.

9. Repeat your mark & feed until you've passed all the treats to your dog, as long as they continue to maintain their impulse control and don't try to grab the treats.

10. If they go to grab the treats at any point, go back to closing your hand.

11. Repeat this exercise a few times in quite a short space of time and you should start to notice that as soon as you offer your hand to your dog, they will either back off or not even bother to sniff your hand, and will remain self controlled even when you open it, at this point they have sussed it! They know in order to get the treats they must leave the treats.

12. You can also integrate the same exercise into games with toys if your dog is toy motivated.

13. Choose a toy they like, place it on the floor, if your dog dives to get it, cover it with your hand, again saying nothing, this is a self control exercise, we want them to figure out for themselves that grabbing for the toy makes it unavailable.

14. When they back away, uncover it again, repeat by covering it if they keep going to grab it.

15. Once they back away, and stay away or maybe they sit, THAT is your MARK POINT, throw the toy or pick it up and have a game of tug with them.

16. You can then play fetch and repeat the exercise randomly throughout the game, or incorporate 'drop it' exercises into your game, then practise the impulse control exercise once more.

Teaching Impulse Control On Lead - Step by Step

1. Have your dog on a normal length lead (4-6ft) and avoid doing this exercise on slippery flooring.

2. Put something desirable down in a room or in your garden, it must be something your dog wants, but not so high value that they will be desperate to get it, treats/toys but not their favourite ones *TIP*: *Put the treats on a plate so they're clearly visible.*

3. You could have someone hold your dog whilst you place the object, or leave them inside while you place the object outside or in another room.

4. With the lead quite short (only a couple of feet) but not taught so you're restraining your dog, start walking toward the item.

5. **The instant** your dog gets ahead of you (even if the lead hasn't gone tight yet) stop walking and bring them to a slow stop. (Refer to lead techniques)

6. There is no cue word for this behaviour, we want our dogs to self learn, so say nothing as you stop.

7. Wait for them to check in (look at you to see why you've stopped) > praise 'good boy/girl' then using your body language and a hand signal, invite them back to your side, and immediately start walking slowly toward the desirable object again.

8. To begin with, especially if your dog is struggling, you could mark and reward for every step they take by your side, to help them get the idea of the game and make it less frustrating.

9. Continue to mark & treat with each step your dog takes with you.

10. If your dog lunges forward, **stop instantly using slow stop.** Your dog needs to learn that any tension in the lead results in the end of forward movement. **This must be consistent** otherwise you will find yourself doing this stop /start for a very long time!

11. If they continue to lunge forward, start to back up slowly as soon as you stop – but be careful not to jerk them on the lead, this is purely to communicate that this behaviour makes the desirable object become less available. You could also spend more time practising the 1 Step at a Time loose lead foundation exercise prior to this one, to make it easier for your dog to understand.

12. Continue to back away from the object until your dog returns to your side to catch up with you, then **immediately** start walking forward again, praising and marking/rewarding as they take any steps with you.

13. As they walk with you, mark & treat, mark & treat, mark & treat. It's much easier and faster for our dogs to learn by giving this rapid consistent feedback to let them know they're doing great, rather than keep letting them fail by pulling ahead and then trying to get them back.

14. Once your dog can walk nicely to the desirable object, they can have it, eat it, or if it's a toy, have a game with them as a reward.

15. Change the object and repeat the exercise.

16. ***Possible Problem:*** If your dog stands at the end of the lead and doesn't look back at you,

    a. Shuffle slowly backwards - the sound should hopefully elicit that look back

    b. Make a little noise (to give them a clue what you want)

    c. Use a higher value treat as the reward (reinforcer)

    d. Use a lower value object/treat to approach, one they won't be so excited about

17. Once your dog can walk up to several low value objects/treats without pulling (this should only take a day or so if working on 3 - 4 short sessions per day) start to reduce the frequency of the treat rewards you give while approaching the object. Use praise to maintain the behaviour, but the reward now is that they get to move forward to the 'prize.'

18. **TIP:** *If the prize is a low level treat or a toy, have some high value treats in your pocket that you can give them when they arrive at the object without pulling, this will increase the value of the behaviour without the need to be treating the whole time you're approaching.*

19. Once your dog is really good at this at home or in the garden, start increasing the value of the objects you're using, so start using favourite toys, favourite yummy treats (leftover chicken / beef / lamb / ham / cheese etc. real yummy smelly stuff)

20. You can now also start to practise out on walks, with life rewards, to help generalise the behaviour and make sure your dog learns that patience wins all sorts of things. For example...

    a. If your dog pulls you to sniff something > slow stop > wait for check in > release to 'Go Sniff' (no treats are required because this is a life reward)

    b. If your dog see's a buddy on their walk and starts to pull to get to them > slow stop > wait for check in > release to 'Go See' or 'Go Play'.

Your Challenge List for Impulse Control Exercises

As always, remember to leave out any of these challenges if they are trigger situations that could cause an emotional outburst, until you've had time to do the necessary reactivity foundation exercises and counter conditioning required. You could, however, work on the impulse control exercises at a distance your dog feels comfortable with, and so can remain calm, and then ask for 'Let's go' so you're not getting too close to the situation.

Can your Dog...	Yep! My dog can do that
Maintain their impulse control for a whole handful of treats	
Maintain their impulse control for one of their toys	
Walk nicely on lead to a tub of treats on the floor	
Walk nicely on lead to one of their toys on the floor	
Walk nicely on lead to a favourite person at home	

Can your Dog...	Yep! My dog can do that
Walk nicely on a lead towards a doggie friend (then be released to 'go play')	
Walk nicely on a lead towards a stranger on a walk	
Add your own challenges...	

Teaching LEAVE IT

Why Teach 'Leave it'

- ✓ Enables you to give a clear communication to your dog when you need them to disengage from something in the environment
- ✓ Helps your dog learn to exhibit self control
- ✓ Teaches your dog how to make better choices around impulsively desirable situations

This behaviour once learnt can be incredibly powerful, and for me is an essential skill for keeping our dogs under control and safe when out walking. It enables us to allow our dogs more freedom and truly enjoy their walks, safe in the knowledge that we can prevent them engaging in behaviours that may cause them harm or place them in danger.

Points to Remember

✓ Be very positive, relaxed and inviting throughout these exercises, some dogs can find learning to disengage from things they want pretty hard work. If you can help make this easier for them, by being very inviting and fun at the right moments during these sessions, the learning process will be more enjoyable.

✓ Only short sessions, take a break, have a play, another short session etc.

✓ If your dog walks off, end the session, have a little game & try again a little while later. (This could be their way of saying that they're feeling a bit stressed out and need a little break)

✓ Never give your dog the treat/object you ask them to leave.

This may seem like a lot of work, but trust me when I say, most dogs not only love learning this exercise once they get the hang of it, but also progress through quite quickly. It just looks a lot because I wanted to make sure I made the teaching instructions as detailed as possible for you.

Stage 1 - Establishing a 'Leave it' Behaviour & Adding a Cue Word

1. Using a medium value food treat, hold it in an enclosed fist in front of your dogs nose.

2. Allow your dog to try to get the treat from you by pushing/nibbling/licking. (No cue word yet)

3. When they give up trying to get the treat (They look away / back away / stop nibbling) THAT is your CLICK POINT, so you click or mark that moment and give a HIGH LEVEL treat from your treat bag or pocket. **Not the treat from your hand**.

4. No words are necessary at this stage. You don't need to speak to your dog at all, just let them work out for themselves what they need to do, they will learn faster that way.

5. Repeat this for 2-3 minutes or use a fixed number of treats, then take a break for 5-10 minutes.

6. Repeat this teaching exercise a few times in quite a short space of time and you should start to notice that as soon as you offer your dog the treat, they will either back off, look away, look down or not even bother to sniff your hand, you know at this stage they have sussed it! They know in order to get a reward they must leave that treat in your hand.

7. ***Possible Problems:***

    a. If your dog doesn't even try to get your 'Leave it' food treat > use a higher level food (smellier, tastier) or maybe they're distracted? If so choose a quieter location or reduce any distractions.

    b. If your dog starts to get really pushy / bullying / chewing your hand > put the treat away and try using a lower value food treat, maybe just some of your dogs own food or dry biscuit.

    c. IMPORTANT NOTE. If your dog shows any signs of becoming aggressive during this exercise, stop the exercise and contact a behaviour consultant.

8. Once you know your dog is deliberately choosing to 'leave' the treat in your hand, then you can start to add your cue word. The cue word is given at the same time as you hold out the treat in your closed fist, and it would be good practise to get into the habit of always saying your dog's name followed by 'leave' or 'leave it'.

    IMPORTANT NOTE: When you say your cue word, make sure you say it in a normal pleasant tone of voice, much the same as you might say it to a child. Your dog hasn't done anything wrong, we're **asking** them to leave the treat. If you get into the habit of shouting your leave it request, or saying it in a cross voice, you may create a negative association for your dog around this exercise. If that happens, it could affect how well they learn, how much they enjoy this interaction with you and so how willing they are to work with you to learn this safety exercise, all of which could ultimately affect how successful it turns out to be in the real world, and we need this to be pretty spot on, it could literally save your dog's life one day.

9. So as you hold out the treat in your closed fist, say '<Fido> Leave it' in a normal tone and if you've waited until you know your dog understands the game, they shouldn't even be trying to get the treat at this point, mark it and reward from your treat bag/pocket as before.

YOUR GOAL FOR THIS STAGE: To issue your 'leave it' cue and have your dog leave the treat completely.

Stage 2 - Adding an Automated Default to Guardian (Look at You)

1. The ultimate aim for this exercise out in the real world, is for us to be able to ask our dogs to disengage (leave) something and look at us for further instruction, so this is the part of the process where we build in the 'look at us' element.

2. Once your dog is really good at stage one, we can now ask for a little more from them, so this time, you're going to repeat the exercise exactly the same as when you finished at stage one. Offer treat in closed fist.... '<Fido> Leave it' .... but now you're going to withhold the click or mark, until your dog actually looks up at your face.

3. Most dogs, when the click or 'Yessss!' marker doesn't come as they expected, will look at you as if to say 'hey where's my click?' and THAT is your new CLICK POINT lots of praise, smile! (Our dogs love it when we smile!) and reward as before, with your higher value treat from your treat bag or pocket.

4. ***Possible Problems:***

   a. If your dog doesn't look up at your face when you withhold the click, make sure you're nice and relaxed and giving your 'leave it' request in a pleasant neutral tone. We can sometimes look a bit intense when we're teaching this exercise, and this can come across negatively to our dogs.

   b. Give your dog a clue - Make a very slight squeak or sniff or kissy noise, move your head slightly into their eye line and they will normally look, then you can click/mark, praise & reward.

   c. Repeat with your clue another 2 or 3 times, then see if they can do it without the clue.

   d. Be prepared to WAIT for your dog to work things out, don't be too hasty in assuming they're not going to do it. Just sit and wait for quite a few seconds and see what happens, you'll be amazed at how quick they can problem solve when we don't interfere!

5. Most dogs cotton on to this very quickly, some dogs however, can find looking directly at our face uncomfortable. If this is the case with your dog, you can mark & reward for glances in your general face direction, you can also make sure your head is turned slightly away from them, making it more comfortable for them to look at you.

6. Repeat the exercise with plenty of short sessions until your dog is doing this really well before moving on to the next stage.

YOUR GOAL FOR THIS STAGE: To give your 'leave it' request and have your dog ignore the treat and look at you.

Stage 3 - Strengthening the New Behaviour & Generalising to All Locations

Once you know your dog understands stage 2 of the game and is reliably looking away from your hand and back to your face, start to practise in different locations.

- ✓ Practise in different rooms of the house
- ✓ Practise it with distractions in the house - people in the room/things going on
- ✓ Practise it out in your garden
- ✓ Practise it out on a walk (a very familiar walk where your dog won't be too distracted)

Stage 4 - Transferring the Behaviour to the Floor

1. The next stage is to place your hand on the floor with the 'leave it' treat underneath it.

2. As you put your hand down, say your dog's name and give your 'leave it' cue (in a pleasant tone)

3. As before, wait for your dog to back off your hand and look at you - then mark & treat from your pocket or treat bag.

4. Most dogs understand the game pretty well by now, and cotton on quickly, but if they take a while to start with, because we've changed the game a bit, you can give them a little clue the first couple of times, by making a sniffy / kissy noise to get that look up to you.

5. Once your dog is doing well with that part of the exercise, you can slowly start to uncover the treat on the floor, and give your 'leave it' request, but remain with your hand close by to cover it again if they try to grab it!

6. Repeat 3 or 4 times then take a break, remember to pick up your 'leave it' treat from the floor as you finish each session.

7. By taking regular breaks, it gives you the opportunity to put the 'leave it' treat down in a new place each time, helping to generalise the behaviour for your dog.

8. Repeat these sessions until you can place a treat on the floor > say '<Fido> leave it' > and your dog will immediately look to you without attempting to get the treat on the floor.

9. Once your dog can do this, place the treat on the floor, give your 'leave it' request and stand up.

10. If your dog tries to take the treat cover it with your foot.

11. Wait until they look up at you - mark, praise & treat from your pocket or treat bag.

12. Don't allow your dog to take the treat from the floor, although sometimes they're super quick and it happens by accident, but don't worry, just reset and start again, or maybe start with the treat under your foot, and then you can uncover it as you say 'leave it' - just make sure your dog has seen it before you ask them to 'leave it'.

13. Repeat this exercise in various rooms around the house.

14. Remember you want to try and say 'Leave it' just once and wait for your dog to respond, the more they can work things out for themselves without prompting, the stronger the behaviour should be.

15. Also remember, your dog is never allowed to get the 'leave it' item, as you finish each session, pick it up and remove it.

YOUR GOAL FOR THIS STAGE: To be able to place a desirable treat on the floor and have your dog ignore it and look at you instead.

Stage 5 - Establishing Reliability with Different Objects

The Training Set up for Stage 5

✓ Make a list of objects your dog finds desirable, or get creative in making up interesting things they may alert to. Start with least desirable objects to set your dog up for success.

✓ You could use things like smelly treats in a tub, treats or human food on a plate, children's toys, socks, tissues, shoes, TV Remotes, plastic bottles etc.

✓ Remember your dog is never allowed to have the item you've asked him to leave, so I would avoid using their own toys for this exercise.

✓ If you find your dog is struggling with any of the stages when you change objects or location, go back to the previous stage and do a few repetitions there before carrying on, to refresh their memory.

✓ Your dog will need to be on a lead for this stage when you start practising outside.

Stage 5 - Step by Step

1. Repeat the exercise in the same way as you did with Stage 4, but this time using your ordered list of desirable objects, starting with the least desirable, and also change the locations you practise in, starting with different rooms around the house, then the garden or out the front of your house, before progressing to out in the real world.

2. If you find it difficult to put an object down whilst holding your dog on the lead, you could put the objects outside first, then take your dog out to practise the exercise.

3. When you start this training outside, you will obviously need to have your dog on a lead, and it's likely they will notice the object from a fair distance away, so you have to be focused, and spot straight away the moment they alert and respond instantly giving your 'leave it' request, bringing them to a slow stop (without yanking/jerking - see lead techniques) so they don't get too close to the object and are able to lunge or pull you to grab it.

4. Remember your cue '<Fido> Leave it' is given in a neutral tone, not a cross tone.

5. As soon as they look back at you, even if it takes a moment while they think about it, MARK IT & REWARD then immediately start SHUFFLING BACKWARDS QUICKLY encouraging them to come after you, then you can REWARD AGAIN with a second treat as they get to you.

   NOTE: This double treat is important as you progress through, because what we're aiming for is our dogs to disengage and then immediately be reconnected with us. So building in the repetition of receiving the second treat, teaches them to start expecting it, which helps to strengthen the sequence of the behaviour.

6. You can immediately walk back towards the object again and repeat the exercise, enabling 3-4 repetitions before finishing.

7. ***Possible Problem:*** If your dog isn't interested in your desirable item

    a. Change the item for something they will definitely show interest in.

    b. Use a quieter location or remove any distractions.

8. ***Possible Problem:*** If your dog keeps lunging and trying to grab the item

    a. Change the item for something less interesting.

    b. Bring your dog to a slow stop a bit further away from the object.

    c. Use higher value rewards

9. ***Possible Problem:*** If your dog doesn't respond, but instead strains on the lead to get the object

    a. Use a less desirable item.

    b. Use higher value rewards

    c. Ensure you use the lead release technique or lead stroking, to encourage your dog to release the tension in the lead.

    d. Try shuffling your feet to give them a clue and elicit the look back.

    e. Try moving into their eye line to elicit the look back, you can then mark and reward - remember to shuffle backwards to make it a more fun & rewarding experience.

YOUR GOAL AT THIS STAGE: To be able to place any desirable object in front of your dog and have them disengage with it and look back to you.

Once you've reached this stage, you can start to integrate this training into your walks and home environment. This is not the complete structured process for a proofed 'Leave it' behaviour, but this should certainly give you enough of a foundation to be able to use in day to day life.

If you have a dog with reactivity issues, or you require a higher degree of impulse control, you may be interested in completing the whole 'Cease & Desist' course, details of which you can find on the website at www.thedogspov.com.

Your Challenge List of Desirable Objects for Your Dog to Leave

Can your Dog Leave...	Yep! My dog can leave that indoors	Yep! My dog can leave that outside
Treats on a plate or in a tub		
Human food on a plate or in a tub		
Socks/Underwear		
Children's Toys		
Hats (*Does everyone's dogs go mad for hats or is it just mine?*)		
TV Remotes		
Add Your Own Challenges...		

Teaching LET'S GO!

Why Teach a 'Let's Go!' Behaviour

- ✓ Gives your dog a clear communication 'We're leaving!' and that you need them to follow you, even if they're busy doing something else

- ✓ Enables you to teach your dog to be comfortable with slight lead pressure

- ✓ Once learnt and practised, it enables you to manoeuvre your dog out of tricky situations quickly and effectively without pulling or dragging them away, an essential skill for reactive dog guardians.

- ✓ Enables you to provide your dog with a clear communication that says 'I've got this, come with me and I'll keep you safe' which can be especially effective when handling reactive dogs.

By teaching and practising 'Let's go' in a really positive and fun way, you're able to build this behaviour as something very constructive for your dog to focus on doing (remember the positive brain focus I mentioned before) which is especially important for fearful or reactive dogs, but equally as useful for just being able to let your dog know when you need to move on, eliminating the need for any pushing, pulling or manhandling of them.

Teaching Let's Go - Step by Step - Stage 1

1. With your tasty treats in your pocket / treat bag and your dog on a normal length lead (4-6ft)

2. Have your happy face and your upbeat attitude with you ☺

3. Start somewhere quiet with no distractions, either at home or in the garden, somewhere very familiar.

4. Take out a tasty treat, show it to your dog as you take a nice happy bouncy step away from them saying in a very upbeat light tone '<Fido> Let's Go!'

5. If the situation has been set up right, your dog should follow the treat and move with you, THAT is your CLICK POINT mark and treat, lots of praise!

6. Repeat this 3 or 4 more times with the treat lure in your hand, then remove it, just asking for the '<Fido> Let's go' as you bounce & step away. Your dog should be up on the game now and will move with you, mark and treat, lots of praise for doing it without the lure.

7. Repeat another 5 or 6 times in different directions without the treat lure, making sure your movement is very upbeat and bouncy each time (dogs love upbeat and bouncy!) marking, treating and praising as they step with you.

8. End the session there or take a break for a little bit, before your dog gets bored, release them to go play and let them know they did great with some big fuss and tickles, maybe even a little chase game.

9. Repeat the whole exercise again with 8-10 treats (you shouldn't need to start with the lure this time) to make sure your dog is moving well with you before you go on to stage 2.

Teaching Let's Go - Step by Step - Stage 2

1. Now you can start taking more steps as you ask your dog to 'Let's go!'

2. Again, still in a quiet environment for the moment.

    a. practise 'Let's go' moving from room to room in your house

    b. practise 'Let's go' coming in from the garden

    c. practise 'Let's go' as you take your dog out the door for a walk

3. Using the same set up as in stage 1 - <Fido> 'Let's go!' in a nice upbeat tone as you bounce away from them. Make sure you're moving as you give the request, this helps your dog learn that these words mean YOU are moving and they are to follow.

4. You can also now start moving away in different directions

    a. sometimes move ahead as you say 'Let's go!'

    b. sometimes move away to the side

    c. sometimes do a u-turn (especially important to practise if you have a reactive dog)

5. Keep your sessions short to prevent boredom, 5-10 treats then end with plenty of praise and tickles to let your dog know they did great!

Teaching Let's Go - Step by Step - Stage 3

1. Once your dog is doing this really well at home and in the garden, which usually only takes a day or two, you can start taking this game on the road.

2. Remember, always start to move AS you give your '<Fido> Let's go!' request.

3. Practise 'Let's go' on your walks, it can be dropped in at all sorts of times...

    a. Say 'Let's go!' when your dog has been sniffing for some time and you need to move on

    b. Say 'Let's go!' after you have waited at a curb, as you cross the road

    c. Say 'Let's go!' after you have stopped to have a chat to a friend or neighbour

4. But also practise 'Let's go' sometimes for no reason, as you're walking along, move away to the side, or drop in a U-turn. By doing this you get lots of opportunities to practise in a fun way and the behaviour becomes really strong and something your dog learns to respond to brilliantly.

Teaching Let's Go - Step by Step - Stage 4

The final stage in this exercise is to practise your 'Let's go' exercise AWAY from distractions. By doing this at times when you don't actually **need** to, at a distance **you** choose so you know your dog will be able to respond, you're able to really proof the behaviour. This means, when you do need it, in a potentially negative or highly distracting situation, you and your dog will be well rehearsed and far more likely to be able to get yourselves out of there!

Using exactly the same process as before, you move AS you say <Fido> Let's go!' practise in real life situations out on your walks with the following challenges, you could move to the side or do a U-turn, just make sure the space you're moving into is clear. ☺

NB: If any of these are actual triggers for your dog, leave them until later down the list, and make sure you start at a nice comfortable distance away.

Your Let's Go Challenge List

Can Your Dog do a 'Let's Go...	Yep! My Dog Can Do That
As you walk towards people	
As you walk towards children playing	
As you walk towards a cyclist	
As you walk towards a scary bin bag (or other strange object)	
As you walk towards another dog	
As you walk towards birds/squirrels/rabbits	
Add your own challenges...	

Teach Your Dog to 'TOUCH' With Their Nose

Why teach your dog to 'Touch' with their nose

- ✓ Touch can be used as a visual cue to build reliable recall responses

- ✓ Touch can be used as an anchor to help regain attention and give an anxious/stressed dog something to focus on, other than their anxiety

- ✓ Touch can be used to help manoeuvre your dog around instead of pulling on their collar

- ✓ Touch can be used to give your dog something to focus on and help position them when at the vets

- ✓ Touch can be used to give your dog a point of focus when teaching Loose Lead Walking

- ✓ Touch can be a great confidence building exercise

- ✓ Touch can be used to teach fun and useful tricks, like shutting cupboard doors, showing you where the treat/food cupboard is when it's dinner time, teaching your dog to 'Jump for Joy' and lots more

Depending on what you want to use your 'Touch' exercise for, you could teach your dog to touch your hand or touch a target, like a target stick or particular item. For this step by step guide I am using my hand as the target, but if you want to use something else, just substitute that in place of where it says hand.

Step 1 - Teaching the Basic Touch

1. Rub a smelly treat on your hand so it smells good to your dog.

2. Hold your hand out to the side of your dogs nose, quite close - just an inch or two away to start with, so it's close enough for them to get a whiff of the smell, but far enough that they have to move their nose to sniff your hand.

3. At the exact moment your dogs nose touches your hand, THAT is your 'CLICK POINT' or Yessss! Point followed by a treat.

4. Timing is important, you must click/mark as your dogs nose bumps your hand.

5. Also be careful you don't move your hand onto your dogs nose - we want your dog to be deliberately choosing to bump your hand, otherwise they won't understand or learn exactly what it is they're doing, because they're not actually doing anything. ☺

6. Repeat this 5 or 6 times, then take a short break (just a few minutes)

7. ***Possible Problem:*** If your dog doesn't touch your hand with their nose

    a. Is your hand too far away? Move it nearer.

    b. Does your dog like what you have rubbed on your hand? Use something smellier/tastier.

    c. Do you have treats in your other hand? Are they staring at those instead - Put your treats in your pocket or on a counter next to you.

    d. Is the environment too distracting? Move somewhere with less distractions.

    e. Try moving your hand slightly up and down (not towards your dog's nose) or wiggling your fingers gently, to catch their eye.

    f.   Most dogs find this exercise easy, but if your dog is struggling, you can mark for any small movements towards your hand. A look to start with - mark that - a slight head move - mark that - and build up from there.

8. After your short break, start again, doing exactly the same thing - If your dog touches your hand first time you can now start putting your hand in different positions, so they have to deliberately move a bit more to touch it.

    a.   Lower it down a bit.

    b.   Have it slightly further away (not too far all at once though)

    c.   On the other side of their face.

    d.   Use your other hand.

    e.   If they're comfortable with it - over the top of their nose so they have to reach up to bump.

9. Once you know your dog is deliberately seeking out your hand to nose bump it, begin adding a cue word to the behaviour. **At the moment your dogs nose bumps, say 'Touch'** mark/reward. At this stage, we're pairing the word with the behaviour, so we say it at the same time that the behaviour happens. Once you have repeated this over a couple of sessions, and your dog is doing really well, you can start to say the word as you offer your hand, making it a cue your dog will now respond to.

10. Repeat this over several more sessions in different rooms around the house, to make sure your dog knows the game well.

11. Once your dog is doing this really well at home, start having little practise sessions on your walks.

12. If your dog can respond to your 'Touch' game on walks - you're both ready for the next stage.

The next stage will depend on what you want to use your 'Touch' behaviour for, but I usually recommend working on both eventually. Choose from the next steps below...

Touch for Recall

Once you have your basic 'Touch' behaviour in place, these are the next steps to start building it as your visual recall cue.

1. Start adding movement to your 'Touch' request - begin at home for a session or two to make sure your dog has the hang of the new element to the game. Once they do, you can start practising it on your walks as well.

2. As you offer your hand and give your '<Fido> Touch' request **- begin slowly backing away so your dog has to follow & move toward you to bump your hand.** The CLICK/MARK POINT is when they bump your hand as before, praise & reward.

3. Repeat this a few times moving slowly backwards in a straight line away with your hand out to your side - inviting your dog to follow you and go for the 'Touch.'

4. Once you've done this over a session or two, and your dog is doing well:

   a. You could start backing away more quickly adding an element of fast movement fun to the game.

   b. You could start moving your hand in a sweeping movement around your body, so your dog follows it.

   c. You could start raising it, in very small increments, higher above their head to teach a 'Jump for Joy' trick - although this has nothing to do with recall, if you have a dog that likes to jump up, this adds a really fun element to this exercise which helps embed that 'Touch' word firmly in their minds as something REALLY fun, meaning when they hear it.... they come running!

   d. **IMPORTANT NOTE:** Please be careful if your dog is older, or has any injuries or ailments that may cause them pain if they jump up, best not to teach this element if they do.

5. When your dog is doing this well at home, time to integrate it into your walks.

   a. Practise in a variety of locations.

   b. Start with lower distraction places to begin with.

   c. Build up to playing this game in more distracting areas.

   d. Drop in a random couple of 'Touch' rehearsals often throughout your walk.

   e. Practise & repetition builds muscle memory = your dog will respond more reliably. If you only use this behaviour when you ACTUALLY need to call your dog away from something, it's unlikely to work.

6. Gradually increase the distance your dog has to travel to 'Touch' but make sure you do this in small increments, and if necessary have your dog on a long line to prevent them running off.

Touch For Redirection or As an Anchor

If you want to focus more on using 'Touch' as a redirection technique or as an anchor to regain attention and act as a focus point for your dog, the challenge list will help you build up the strength and reliability of your 'Touch' behaviour. If you add a sustained hand touch, this will also enable you to use touch to manoeuvre your dog.

Teach a Sustained Hand Touch

All this means is teaching your dog to be able to 'Touch' your hand for an extended amount of time. This basically just involves delaying your click/mark in very small increments each time, so your dog will hold their nose against your hand for longer and longer.

Once they can do that, you can start to move with them touching your hand, again gradually to start with, let them get the hang of the new game and then slowly build up the distance they will walk along touching your hand.

Have your dog on a long line/lead if necessary, if you think they will just wander off sniffing. Obviously if you have a reactive dog, and any of these things are triggers for them, you need to practise your 'Touch' training a lot before introducing these triggers, and then you need to start at a comfortable distance from the trigger distraction to ensure your dog will be able to respond without reacting.

Practise & Generalisation Challenge List for Touch

Can Your Dog do a 'Touch' (Or a Sustained Hand Touch)	Yep! My Dog Can Do That
At home with people/other dogs around	
In the garden	
When you first leave the house to go for a walk	
Randomly on a street walk	
Randomly on a field walk	
When children are playing nearby	
When other dogs are in view	
When people are walking past you	
When dogs are walking past you	
When a jogger runs past	
When there is traffic going past	
When a cyclist/motorbike goes past	
Add your own challenges...	

Teaching Your Dog an Awesome RECALL

Obviously I don't need to put why it's important for us to teach our dogs a reliable recall behaviour, but what I do just want to emphasise here is that, for the most part, the number one reason recall behaviour fails to work when you really need it to, is because most people don't practise it anywhere near enough.

This is especially true of puppy guardians. When you first get your puppy, you are their world, you are their universe, you are everything to them and they trot about and follow you everywhere, coming instantly when called, even when at the park and out on walks.

I can't tell you the number of times a client, who's little puppy is between 8 and 16 weeks old has said to me 'Oh yep he/she's got a great recall', but unfortunately this lulls people into a false sense of security, and they stop practicing recall, they stop testing it, they stop rewarding it, and this is where the problems begin.

As soon as the puppy reaches around five to six months of age (it can vary slightly between breeds / sex etc) suddenly their recall is not so good. They start running off to see people or dogs, they start chasing things and not coming back, they start ignoring you and continuing to sniff, or wander off and simply do their own thing. Welcome to your teenager! ☺

I'm not going to go into all the reasons why your recall becomes less reliable at this point, so all I will say, to keep this as succinct and to the point as possible, is that teaching your dog a strong reliable recall exercise requires practise, practise and more practise. Practise through puppyhood and **especially** the teenage period, and even beyond that at a maintenance level in some cases.

Management is another huge area of teaching your dog a reliable recall, so be prepared to get them back on a long training line (not retractable) attached to a secure harness and do more recall rehearsals if they start choosing to head off and do their own thing at any point. That way you can prevent them practising the behaviour of NOT coming back to you and getting great rewards for that behaviour, with all the fun things they find to do by themselves! Remember I said the behaviours our dogs practise the most become the strongest?

The biggest mistake many guardians make when first starting recall training is to give the cue word BEFORE the behaviour is happening, BEFORE their dog has learnt what the cue word means. In order for your dog to associate your recall word with the behaviour you want - come back to me - your dog has to actually be doing the behaviour of running toward you AS you say the word.

So, if you can imagine your dog learns by association, if your dog doesn't already know what the recall word means, and you say <Fido Come> when they are sniffing in the garden.... Fido will associate the word 'Come' with the behaviour of 'Sniffing in the garden' ... Are you with me?

Recall Teaching Tips

- ✓ Always use the same word for your recall (unless it becomes poisoned in some way)
- ✓ Always have fun when teaching recall, you're going to be in direct competition with some heavy duty environmental reinforcers (squirrels, dogs, people, balls, stinky stuff to roll in etc)
- ✓ Use high value rewards (treats or toys)
- ✓ Practise your recall exercises before your dog is fed, or the chances are your tasty treats won't be high value enough to compete with all the other stuff your dog finds interesting.

Teaching Recall - Step by Step

This is the basic process for installing your dogs recall behaviour. Once you have the basics going on, it's simply about rehearsing a lot! Practising in different locations and with different distractions, but **always with the situation managed** and in a way that helps them succeed, this is the part that many people don't realise or forget to practise and is often the reason recall never becomes a nice strong, reliable behaviour.

1. I know this may be obvious, but before working on your recall training, you need to have practised the name game well enough that your dog is likely to respond at least most of the time.

2. Decide on your recall word or sound (whistle perhaps, but what will you do if you forget your whistle?) and make sure everyone uses the same word or sound when out with your dog.

3. Have some tasty treats in your pocket or a treat bag and start this exercise at home, in a quiet room.

4. Say your dog's name only <Fido> and then do anything that will get them moving toward you, things like:

a. shuffling away quickly, sideways on with inviting body language

b. patting your legs

c. jumping up & down

d. making a little excited squeaky noise

5. AS your dog starts moving toward you THEN you say your recall word, not before. To begin with the recall word must be heard WHILE they are doing the behaviour we want.

6. Give plenty of verbal praise + your recall word on the way 'Good boy, here, gooood boy, here.'

7. As they reach you THAT is your MARK POINT give several treats and lots of praise.

8. At this stage don't ask them to sit or do anything else, you can add that in later if you want to, when they have a great recall in all sorts of locations, for now, we just want them to come running!

9. Repeat for 10 treats then take a break.

10. Practise again a short while later for another 10 treats.

11. Take a break.

12. Practise again a short while later for another 10 treats. Remember make it Fun Fun Fun ☺

13. If all is going well, you can now start using your recall word to actually call your dog to you, so still in your quiet location at home or in the garden '<Fido> Here' (or whatever word you have chosen) start shuffling /moving and they should respond in the same way as they have been. Praise on the way, MARK as they arrive, reward.

14. By now your dog should be loving this game and you can start practising in slightly more distracting areas around the home.

15. When you start recalling your dog to you from other locations around the home and garden, at times they may not be able to see you initially, so wait until they're in view then show them your excitement by moving away from them, patting your leg & giving lots of encouraging praise on the way.

16. Remember to always mark & reward when they arrive.

17. At this stage you can also randomly touch your dogs collar as you reward them, if you remember to do this regularly, you shouldn't end up with a dog that darts away from you when you reach to take hold of them out in the real world.

Work through the following challenges before taking your recall to the next level.

Your Challenge List for Basic Recall Exercises

Although this may look like a lot of work for just the first stage, this is the foundation that all your other recall exercises will be built on. It should actually only take a day or two at the most to have your dog at a stage they should be ready to succeed at these challenges.

Challenge: Will Your Dog Recall and Come to You...	Yep! My Dog Can Do That
In a quiet room with no one around	
In the house when other family members are there	
From one room in the house to another	
From inside the house out into the garden	
From the garden into the house	
When they're playing a game with other family members	

Being called away when playing with other family members may be a tricky one, so set your dog up for success by being quite close to them when you start practising this one. Have something mega tasty for when they reach you, praise massively then tell them to go play again, or play with them yourself, double bubble reward!

Games that can help you strengthen your Recall behaviour

The following games are a great way to have fun playing (practising) recall out and about on your walks. I recommend you play them at least once during every walk you go on, and if it's a longer walk, I would drop these games in randomly throughout the walk.

Ping Pong Recall

1. You will need two people on a walk to play this game. Have your dog trailing a long line if necessary, so they can't run off and reward themselves.

2. Starting in a low distraction area – a quiet corner of a park or field with not much going on and after you have allowed your dog to have a sniffy and a wee/poo if they need one.

3. Two people take it in turns to call your puppy/dog back and forth – marking /treating on arrival.

4. Start a short distance apart to begin with, only 10-15ft then gradually increase the distance your dog has to race towards each of you!

5. Call your dog's name, give your recall request '<Fido> Here!' and encourage them to you in any way you like (clapping / shuffling away sideways /squealing noises etc)

6. As your dog approaches, lots of praise during the approach.

7. As your dog/puppy gets better at their recall, you can begin to fade out all the crazy dog person encouragement, I usually still do a little something though, just because it's fun!

8. Only practise this game for short periods on your walk, so you always stop before your dog gets bored, alternate between doggy sniffy time and recall practise, so your dog gets the best of both, because once they have a great recall behaviour on cue, they are going to get so much more freedom!

By playing this game in lots of different locations you will continue to strengthen your dogs recall by being the most fun thing they love to do, and they will be so busy with you, they won't even notice all those other distractions going on.

Hide and Seek Recall

You can play this one at home and on walks, as long as it's safe and you have taken the necessary precautions to make sure your dog won't run off while the hider is hiding!

Ideally in the early stages of recall practise, I would recommend playing this game with two people, so one to hide and the other to keep your dog safe while they look for you. Once your dog starts to get more reliable with their recall, you can play it when you're out on walks by yourself, as long as you're in a safe location and your dog is not likely to run off.

1. One person holds your dog whilst they watch the other person go off and hide in the house/bushes.

2. Release your dog as the hidden person shouts '<Fido> Here!' (or whatever recall cue word you have chosen)

3. When your dog finds the hidden person have a big greeting and celebration of tickles, praise and a jackpot treat reward!

4. Whilst the celebration is going on – the other person goes off to hide, so the dog may not have noticed they've gone, and now they have to hunt for them.

5. I like to play this game both ways, sometimes building that anticipation by having the dog watch the person disappear, sometimes having someone hide while they're not looking, adding that air of mystery to the game, where is that sound coming from?

6. Repeat the game a few times, then take a break or continue on your walk.

7. Drop this game into walks as and when you fancy and your dog's impression of the recall word is now becoming great fun!

8. If you're walking on your own, and it's safe to do so, you could allow your dog to get a little ahead of you, then duck into some bushes or behind a tree and call them. Lots of party praise when they find you!

Distracted Recall Games

You can play distracted recall games both at home and on walks. When on walks you can use environmental distractions, but if you have someone with you, they could create controlled distractions for you to practise with as well.

1. Have your dog on a long line, preferably with a harness.

2. Wait until your dog is distracted by something, starting with low level distractions and nothing that's a major trigger for them, or that gets them highly excited. (That comes later after more practise)

3. Give your recall request '<Fido> Here!' and recall your dog away from the distraction.

4. Use the same process as in the beginning, making yourself interesting by moving or squeaking > Praise & encourage all the way > Mark & reward when they reach you.

5. NOTE: A great way to increase the power of this game is to make it into a Premack recall, if the distraction you're calling your dog away from is something they can have. The Premack recall game is covered in more detail next, but in a nutshell, once your dog reaches you, Mark and then release them to go back to what they were doing.

6. To start with, the distractions you choose must be of low value to your dog so they will leave them and thus get into the habit of responding to your recall request. They won't learn anything by failing, so if you're pretty sure your dog WON'T respond to your recall request, then don't give it, choose a different easier distraction or practise more at easier recall games for longer.

7. ***Possible Problem:*** If your dog won't leave the distraction and return to you

    a. Is the distraction too interesting & high value at this stage?

    b. You could try being further away from the distraction and recalling from there, gradually moving closer.

    c. You could try a distraction that is not so interesting.

    d.   You could try being closer to your dog, so you're only recalling a very small distance to start with, almost running away from the distraction **with** them, then gradually build up your recall distance.

8. Gradually increase the desirability of the distractions you use to recall your dog away from, make sure you always praise and reward heavily if your dog recalls away from something they are really interested in!

9. Obviously you will need to keep your dog on a training line until they're pretty good at their recall, to ensure you set them up for success with the distracted recall exercises. If they're allowed to run off to distractions, even just once and self reward, you could have undone weeks of recall training.

10. You can of course enlist the help of friends or family to distract your dog on purpose, (set up the exercise so you can strengthen it) They can use treats or toys to entice your dog to stay with them, but your dog must never get them... until they run to you following your recall request, then you can either reward them with mega treats and toys that you were hiding behind your back, or run with them back to the other person and YOU give the toys/treats to your dog, so even though they left it to come to you, they end up being rewarded with what they wanted in the first place.

Premack Recall Using a Toy

1. Shorten your lead so you're holding it about a foot from your dogs collar NOTE: Ideally your dog will have a harness on.

2. Keep the lead taught but not super tight, you don't want your dog to be straining against you, this is just to stop them launching forward after the toy and hitting the end of the lead.

3. There is no need for your dog to be in a sit or down - just hold them.

4. Gently throw the toy out in front of your dog.

5. No need to say anything as you throw it, this isn't a leave it exercise.

6. Once you've thrown the toy, start to move away backwards along the lead, keeping it taught, but **not** pulling on your dog, this needs to be a choice they make, not something you make them do, they won't learn anything that way. NOTE: To start with don't move too far, you can build this up gradually increasing your recall distance once your dog has learnt and understood the game.

7. Give your recall word and call your dog to you.

8. They may take a moment to respond in the beginning, looking longingly after their toy, if this is the case you could try:

    a. Shuffling your feet and moving about a bit. Most dogs respond well to movement.

    b. Making a kissy noise to get their attention, as they look start to shuffle away from them inviting them to follow you.

    c. Wave your arms around to catch their peripheral vision.

    d. Move closer to them and repeat your recall word, as you move away to the side, ensuring they can see you and your movement will catch their eye.

9. As soon as your dog gives up looking at the toy and arrives back with you, THAT is your CLICK POINT Mark it and either run with your dog or release them to go get that toy! There is no need to treat here, being released to get the toy is the reward.

10. Depending on what length of lead you're using, be really careful that your dog doesn't jerk themselves on the lead as they run to get their toy, you definitely don't want that happening. So you could...

    a. Use a longer lead or long line.

    b. As you release your dog to go get that toy, run with them to get it, this will prevent them reaching the end of the lead and jerking themselves.

    c. Make sure you don't throw the toy further away than the length of lead you have.

11. So to summarise the process

    a. Short lead

    b. Gently throw toy out

    c. Quickly move backwards to end of lead

    d. Give recall cue

    e. As your dog arrives back to you > MARK it > release / run with to go get toy

    f. Have a game with the toy > drop it > repeat exercise

12. Once your dog knows the game well, you can start increasing the distance you recall them to you before releasing them to get that toy.

13. Once you're able to recall your dog a decent distance, say 20-30ft and they're coming every time, you could start using life rewards to practise this exercise, this will make it a really nice strong reliable behaviour, because your dog gets to have all the fun things in life they want, if they can choose you first. Using the same set up as above to start with, so your dog can't fail, practise your Premack recall:

a. If there are dogs around your dog knows and normally plays with, use a Premack recall and the reward would be getting released to go play with their friends.

b. Getting released to go play with family members.

c. Getting released to go sniff something (this one is particularly useful if you have a dog that tends to drag you to sniffy spots!)

d. When your dog wants to chase small furries (obviously with them on lead, you're going to have to chase with them!)

You can of course also practise this same exercise using treats as the reward, so it would be exactly the same process as laid out above, but you would just toss out some tasty treats instead of a toy, then when you release to go get it, your dog can rush forward and have a wonderful snuffle up of all the treats. Just be careful if you're using treats to practise, that there aren't other dogs nearby that might swoop in and steal the treats, or cause a scuffle over them when your dog is hoovering them up.

A Few Final Points on Teaching a Successful Recall

Never use the training line to 'reel' your dog in, it's purely for use as a prevention to stop them from running off. If you only ever use force to get your dog to return to you, as soon as you aren't there to enforce them, your recall will fail.

The trick with recall is to use whatever you need to, to get your dog to WANT to come back to you. When a dog makes a choice to come back to you instead of going to visit another dog (or do the things they like to do instead of coming back) then you know their recall is starting to become Awesome!

Avoid getting cross or frustrated with your dog for not returning to you. This is one of the best and quickest ways to ruin your dogs recall. If someone was cross or frustrated with you, would you want to run over to them? I'm guessing not, and it's the same for your dog. They will read your body language and negative energy from a long way off, and this can actually prevent them from wanting to come anywhere near you.

Dogs do what is the most rewarding to them, the most fun. Recall training is all about teaching your dog YOU are the most fun/rewarding, whilst PREVENTING them from practising the behaviour of running off to find their own fun (Visiting other people / dogs / chasing squirrels / eating poop etc.) You want to be the provider of all the treats, toys, fun, playing & happy stuff, or at least be included in the decision making process.

Make sure you stay attentive on your walks and notice or actively look for opportunities to practise your recall in real life situations. Use these opportunities to set yourself and your dog up for controlled recall success, these are the situations when recall magic starts to happen.

If your dog fails to respond to your recall, and you can feel yourself getting frustrated, it's fruitless to simply keep repeating your recall request, clearly it's not working so we need to do something different at this time. Take a deep breath and depending on the situation, you have a couple of options.

1. If your dog is not recalling, but isn't running off to see something else either:

   a. See if you can entice them over by doing something silly, a little dance, start laughing, say 'Ooooh what's this' and crouch down, as if looking at something on the ground, so maybe your dog will wonder what you're doing and come to investigate (this helps to reduce your negative energy as well)

   b. When your dog arrives with you, say 'Hi' and sprinkle a few treats on the ground, they may not have responded to your recall but that was a whole 2 minutes ago! You're in a different learning space now, and your dog has chosen to come over, so make it a positive thing for them, as they snuffle up the treats, calmly take them by the collar and clip on their lead or long line.

   c. Now you have them back under control, you can ask them to do something they know well, and then MARK & reward them for that, to make it into a positive experience.

   d. You now have your dog back under control and so will be able to do recall practise exercises without the worry of them running off.

2. If your dog is not recalling and running off to see something, you're obviously going to have to follow them, but try to avoid running after them or chasing them.

   a. Depending on how bad your dog's recall reliability is, it might be that as you get closer, you're able to entice them away with your usual recall practise setup.

   b. Or it may be that you actually need to go and physically get them. Try to keep cool, apologise to anyone as necessary, calmly clip your lead on your dog and move on. Once you're in a quiet space, do some engagement exercises and get your dog reconnected with you and some positivity back in your situation, before continuing your walk. In all honesty, my recommendation if this has happened, is that your dog does not have a reliable enough recall at this stage to be off lead, so more practise with management in place before they are off lead again.

Even after your dog has a reliable recall in place, if for any reason you experience a situation where your dog doesn't come back a few times in a row when there are distractions, pop them back on their long line and go back to doing some recall strengthening exercises, to remind them of how great it is to come back to you when you call them. It could be 6 months later, or even a year or longer. Whenever it is, if you assume this is a one off event, it's likely you could find your dog disappearing off into the distance on an increasingly regular basis. You have been warned! ☺

Your Distracted Recall Challenge List

Challenge: Will Your Dog Recall and Come to You...	Yep! My Dog Can Do That
When you see people walking ahead	
When you see children playing nearby	
When there is another dog in the distance	
When there are other dogs playing ahead	
When you see a cyclist	
When you see horses coming	
Add your own challenges...	

Teaching an EMERGENCY 'STOP!'

Why Teach a 'Stop!' Behaviour

- ✓ Teach your dog to know when you REALLY need them to Stop!
- ✓ Teach your dog to be ok with a harsh tone
- ✓ Prevent your dog from becoming confused in an emergency
- ✓ Show your dog that Stop and Return doesn't always mean the end of fun.

I have used the word stop for this teaching guide, but you can use 'Wait' if you prefer, just make sure you don't use that word for anything else (which I do). We really want it to be clear to our dogs, that when we say this word, they need to STOP!!

Teaching Emergency Stop - Step by Step

The process for teaching this exercise begins with normal, relaxed body language and engaging tone of voice, but once your dog is responding well, we want to gradually include a strong tone into this teaching process. The chances are high, that when you really need this behaviour to work (in an actual emergency) you're automatically going to shout it, and we want our dogs to be comfortable with that.

Many dogs can become a little confused and panicky if we suddenly start shouting and projecting fear or anxiety, this can cause them to either not respond, look for the cause of concern or respond with confusion about what they're meant to do. Your anxious voice may prevent them from wanting to come back to you, and could cause them to run away or disengage, and we absolutely do not want this in an emergency. So we want to teach them to be comfortable when we use a louder, urgent tone of voice, and know that it's still going to be awesome when they get back to us, and that we're not actually cross with them because we will have practised it often before.

Stage 1 - Establishing the 'Stop' Behaviour

1. Begin in a non distracting environment, like your garden or a very low distraction environment, like a quiet field, park or track while out on your daily walk.

2. Have your dog on a normal length lead (4-6ft ideally)

3. With normal, relaxed and soft body language, begin walking forward.

4. As soon as your dog starts to move ahead of you, at this stage just a head and shoulders in front, you say '<Fido> Stop!' in a light but firm tone, so it has a bit of a 'Yip' to it, and encourages your dog to go 'Oooh what was that!' and thus stop and turn to look at you.

5. As soon as they do, THAT is your CLICK POINT mark it with a click or a 'Yessss!' and shuffle backwards slightly, smiling, enticing them to turn toward you. (They don't need to come toward you at this point, but we would like a body turn, as it helps to encourage that engagement with you for whatever you're going to ask for next in the future)

6. As they do this turn, you can step in and reward with several jackpot treats, a surprise tug game or whatever reward your dog would class as awesome! For some it can be simply praise and scratches, but for this exercise to stand up in an emergency, we want to make the reward for our dog REALLY worthwhile right from the beginning, so pull out the big guns for this one! (But remember, don't use your big guns rewards for everything or you could devalue them into little guns!)

7. Make your praise & reward a big deal for a moment, this is not one of those exercises where you just want to be popping a treat in and that's it, we want MEGA memory muscle built up here, so make it count.

8. Once you're done with your praising and rewarding, you can move on and repeat that 2 or 3 more times, before ending the session and continuing on your walk.

9. We don't want to overdo the repetitions for this one so it becomes nagging and boring, so keep sessions nice and short, but remember to practise them frequently.

Stage 2 - Building up Distance

So we have the basic behaviour in place, now we want to start adding some distance to the exercise, because after all, if our dogs were always close by our side, it's unlikely we would need to ask them to stop in the first place. As I'm sure most of us want them to be able to run free and have fun, we need to teach them that stop means stop no matter where you are or what you're doing.

There are a couple of options within this stage of the exercise, and I do recommend you work on both, because we need to consider the kind of scenario's this behaviour would be needed for. So it might be necessary to teach some other exercises, recall and wait/stay, before this one, if you haven't done so already (Although recall is kind of built into this exercise, so it will help build a stronger recall when you practise this anyway)

So we may need our dogs to:

- ✓ **'Stop! & Wait/Stay'**. You may have seen another dog or something concerning behind you, and you don't want your dog running back to you and risking the possibility they will see it, or be drawn into it and run past you. So you just want them to stop and wait/stay in place until you get to them. It may be at that point you need to put them on a lead, or you can release them to "Go Play" again.

- ✓ **'Stop! & Return'**. You may have spotted something up ahead and would like your dog to come back, so you can make sure they're safe and under control. Or you may simply be getting near a road, or car park and you need your dog back with you to be put on a lead.

- ✓ **'Stop! & Release'**. You may just need your dog to stop while you catch up with them a little bit, then you can release them to 'Go Sniff' again. Obviously this just needs a release cue to be learnt.

The process for building up distance is very simple, you just need to keep repeating the exercise as above, but let your dog gradually get further and further in front of you before giving your '<Fido> Stop!' request.

Remember at this stage, when we say 'Stop!' we are still saying it in a 'Yippy' but confident tone, so it helps get our dogs attention and make sure they realise this is a positive game.

1. **For 'Stop & Wait'** you will need to have previously taught your dog how to 'Wait' or 'Stay' on request.

    a. Once you have that exercise taught, the process here becomes '<Fido> Stop!'

    b. As they stop and body turn to look 'Good Boy, Wait, Good Boy, Wait' as you walk towards them.

    c. Then your new MARK POINT is AS you reach them.

    d. Praise & Reward.

2. **For 'Stop and Return'** you will need a basic recall word in place, I use 'Here'

    a. So once you have that, the process becomes '<Fido> Stop!>

    b. As they stop and body turn to look 'Good Boy, Here!'

    c. Immediately smiling and shuffling quickly backwards, enticing them to chase you - plenty of fun energy needed here! Praise as they run toward you 'Good Boy, Good Boy'

    d. Then your new MARK POINT is AS they reach you.

    e. Party praise & Reward.

    f. NB: Make sure that you don't tug on the lead to get them to start coming to you, we want this to be their choice so it becomes a nice strong, reliable response. If you've been practising your basic recall, and you're not in a highly distracting environment, they should immediately start returning to you. Remember, make it count, make it fun, make it memorable! Movement is enticing to dogs, do a little dance if necessary ☺

3. Remember, you're building up distance very gradually, so when you start with these two new options, start with your dog close and gradually let them get further and further in front. If you suddenly let them get 20-30ft ahead, and try either of these options, it might make it more difficult for you both to succeed.

4. I do recommend alternating randomly between the three options of 'Wait' or 'Return' or simply release, so your dog doesn't start anticipating what comes next.

5. Once your dog is doing well with both these options on a shorter length lead, you could progress to having them on a longer 30ft-40ft training line.

6. **PLEASE NOTE**: We do recommend when using long lines to have your dog wearing a harness to prevent any damage to their necks, just in case they shoot off and inadvertently hit the end of the line, but if you keep this exercise in low distraction environments, and build up gradually until your dog is really good at it, that shouldn't happen.

7. So keep repeating the basic exercise, being very conscious of controlling the degree by which you increase the distance, gradually letting them get a bit further and a bit further before giving your 'Stop!' request.

8. When you're getting great responses with all of these options in low distraction environments, and if it's safe to do so, you can start practising this with them off lead, but just be careful that you don't set them up to fail. If they're likely to run off or go off too far ahead of you and distract themselves, this could mean they won't remain connected or listening to you, and so won't respond. If you have worked through the previous exercises, hopefully this won't be the case.

Stage 3 - Adding Distractions

Ok, so now we're going to start teaching our dogs to become good at stopping, even when there are really interesting things around to distract them, this is a key aspect of the process, so make sure you're both working really well together at the previous 2 stages before you move on to this one.

1. To start with, because we're increasing the difficulty here for our dogs, you need to go back to the way we started this exercise in stage 1, by asking your dog to stop when they're only a very small distance in front of you and on a normal length lead.

2. You have two choices here

   a. You can create your own distractions, by placing interesting objects on the floor, thereby keeping a little more control over the whole exercise and the level of the distractions.

   b. You could use real life distractions, but you would still need to make them progressively difficult. So start with something your dog finds mildly interesting, not something they find incredibly interesting! Also with real life distractions, you may find you have greater success and progress faster if you start practising this exercise at a bit of a distance from wherever the distraction is. So for example, if you're using a cyclist as a distraction, don't be stood right next to where they're going to come past, be 10-15ft back and practise at that point, making sure your dog can do it at that distance before gradually moving closer.

3. So as you see a distraction in the distance

   a. Start to walk calmly towards it.

   b. As your dog gets slightly ahead of you, ask for your '<Fido> Stop!' (Yippy tone)

   c. MARK it, praise party & reward.

   d. **Start to walk towards it again.**

   e. As they get slightly ahead of you, '<Fido> Stop!' as they stop 'Good Boy, Wait'

   f. Walk towards them, and only MARK & praise party & jackpot reward as you reach them.

   g. **Start to walk towards it again.**

   h. As they get slightly ahead of you, '<Fido> Stop!' as they stop 'Good Boy, Here!'

   i. Shuffle backwards excitedly, smiling, enticing them to chase.

   j. As they arrive back with you that's your MARK point, praise party & Jackpot Reward!

4. Repeat, Repeat, Repeat. Practise, practise, practise! ☺

5. Once your dog is doing great with this exercise on their shorter lead, you can once again start to let them get further and further in front of you before asking them to stop. (Again we would recommend having them on a long training line until they're pretty reliable at this, otherwise they could run off, self reward and learn nothing)

6. Remember to use different distractions, in different locations and at varying distances to make sure your dog gets reeeeaaaaallly good at 'Stop!' (Your training plan in the Appendix section could be useful here, to help you keep track)

Stage 4 - Adding the Emergency Tone

By now your dogs should be really great at 'Stop!' and be able to Stop and wait or Stop and come back when they're quite a distance from you, and also when there are distractions around that interest them. Keep working on these so this behaviour becomes really strong and reliable. It's great to be able to allow your dog that freedom to wander and just 'be a dog' safe in the knowledge you can prevent them getting themselves into trouble (well 99% of the time, remember where dogs are concerned, there is no such things as 100%)

The last part of the exercise is to add in that strong energy, so our dogs don't become alarmed if we suddenly emit a surge of panic at them and scream 'Stop!' from the top of our lungs.

1. As you continue to practise 'Stop' on your daily walks, start gradually increasing both the volume of your voice and the tone, so it begins to mimic that panic kind of tone you might use in a real life situation.

2. Remember to do this gradually though, and if your dog looks startled at any point, or shows hesitation in returning to you, there's a good chance you may have gone too far too quickly, and they're now unsure about the situation.

3. Just go back to your 'Yippy tone' and start again from there, making sure you build up in very small increments of both tone and volume.

4. Make sure, for Stop & Return, as soon as they look at you, you move! As soon as you move, this not only helps to entice your dog back to you, but it can also serve as a marker point for **you** to shift your energy from panic to fun, thus helping your dog feel the desire to rush back to you.

Use the Stop! Challenge List to Help You

With the following challenges, have your dog on a long line if necessary to start with, to prevent them making a wrong choice. As always, if any of these challenges are triggers for your dog, avoid practising with those until your dogs reactivity has been reduced or you can practise at a distance that keeps them under threshold.

Can Your Dog Stop & Wait or Stop & Return...	Yep! My Dog Can Do That
Out on a walk with no real distractions	
Out on a walk with a person ahead of you	
Out on a walk with a person & a dog ahead of you	
Out on a walk when they see children playing	
Out on a walk with a jogger coming toward you	
Out on a walk when they see a bird, squirrel, pheasant etc.	
Add your own challenges...	

Teaching SETTLE

Why teach your dog a 'Settle' behaviour

- ✓ An excellent exercise for teaching your dog to learn to switch off & relax
- ✓ Helps high energy dogs learn to calm down
- ✓ Useful for anxious dogs who feel the need to follow you everywhere
- ✓ Helps you to manage excessive stress, over arousal & excitement

The training for this exercise will work best if you can choose carefully the time of day you teach it. Most of us know what times of day our dogs are calmer than others, so avoid choosing a time when your dog may be over excited, this would make it harder for them to do and thus slow down the learning process. I would also recommend avoiding a time when your dog is tired or visibly stressed, as this could also inhibit learning.

For example, my dogs are calm after their walk in the mornings, and then settle down for naps, so I might choose to do this exercise when we return from our walk. Around lunchtime, they start to get fidgety as they're well rested and know that it won't be long before we go out again, so I would avoid this time. Again following our afternoon walk, they're generally relaxed and calm, so this could be a good time.

So think about when would be a good time for your particular dog, when they're most likely to be calm and relaxed, willing to settle and receptive to learning. Once you have taught this exercise and your dog has a clear understanding of it, **then** you will be able to start using it to **ask** your dog to settle at times when they may be a bit over excited, but during the learning stages, in order to set them up for success, we want them to be in a 'ready to settle' frame of mind.

I have covered a couple of ways to teach Settle here. The first is free shaping and the second is a more structured teaching approach.

Teaching Settle - Step by Step (Free Shaping Method)

1. So to begin, as you go about your day, at a time when your dog is relaxed and happy and NOT focused on you, reward them, quietly place a treat between their paws and walk away.

2. If they're sitting or laying and staring at you, this doesn't count, because they're still focused on you and expecting something.

3. At first they may instantly get up thinking this is an invitation to interact and if they do, then for the purpose of this self relaxation exercise, simply continue what you were doing, disengage from them and ignore their attempts to interact with you.

4. Wait for them to settle again then praise softly and lay a few treats at their paws.

5. Build up to the point where you can chat to them softly without them needing to get up.

6. If your dog remains relaxed and laid down, reward them again, then walk away and go about what you were doing.

7. Keep practising this exercise at appropriate times, until your dog realises that it's ok to relax and be by themselves, that you will not suddenly escape from the house without them noticing, or that the only time they get your attention is when they're asking for it, or following you everywhere.

Quite often, especially with hyperactive dogs, and dogs with a more demanding nature, we fail to notice when they're just being good, but when they're being annoying or demanding they get our attention, so guess what, being annoying and demanding works well for your dog! We want to let our dogs know that we notice when they're being good sometimes, reducing the likelihood they will feel like the only time they get our attention is when they play up. Funnily enough this kind of exercises works the same with children. ☺

Teaching Settle - Step by Step (Structured Method)

1. Ensure your dog's physical, emotional and mental needs have been met. They have been walked, had some adequate attention time, been fed if necessary etc.

2. Begin indoors, in a quiet room with no distractions. Have your dog with a simple flat collar on and a 6ft lead if you think they will be distracted and wander off or mob you for treats or attention.

3. Have a store of treats to hand, in your pocket or in a treat bag/pot next to you. This exercise will probably work best if you have treats your dog likes, and so will find reinforcing, but not too high value that they get all over excited about them.

4. Holding the end of the lead, take a seat in a chair and relax, you could have a book or magazine to hand to imitate reading, or you could simply sit and look out the window. The point here is not to sit staring at your dog, we want them to notice you visibly relax, which will help to communicate to them that nothing is going to be happening. For some dogs if you sit and look at them, they won't settle down but will instead view this as a 'training' situation and could start offering all sorts of behaviours, or may even start to get frustrated.

5. There is no cue here, you don't need to say anything, just relax. As you disengage, remain aware of what your dog is doing - most dogs, if you have timed this right, will fairly quickly just lay down at your feet. As soon as they do this, take a treat and calmly place it between their paws.

6. You don't need to say anything, praise them or touch them, just place the treat and sit back again.

7. At this point your dog may instantly get up, that's fine, just remain relaxed, disengaged and wait for them to settle again, repeating as above.

8. If your dog remains laying down, count slowly to 5 and then place another treat between their paws. Again say nothing, remaining quiet and relaxed and just place the treat and sit back again.

9. If your dog remains laying down but is staring at you, waiting for the next treat, try to wait until they break that stare, then instantly (but calmly) place another treat between their paws without engaging in eye contact or praising.

10. If your dog continues to lay in his relaxed position, without constantly staring at you, continue counting to 5 and placing a treat in the same way.

11. Repeat this for 1 minute, then look at your dog, praise them calmly and stroke them calmly, get up and move to another spot and repeat the exercise for another minute (you can build up the length of time your dog will remain settled later on, after they understand the exercise completely)

12. If your dog looks tired, you could end the session there and do another one later in the day when they're calm.

13. If your dog drops into a very relaxed state, i.e. they look very soft in their face and body, they have flopped their bottom to the side in a very relaxed position and maybe even laid their head down, you could choose to place a treat, unclip the lead and walk quietly away.

14. When you end this exercise, whether your dog is completely relaxed or not, end it calmly. Smile in their direction, say in a whisper 'good settle' and quietly walk away. Avoid ending the session by giving excited praise and big tickles as this is going to immediately raise their energy and undo all the calmness of the settle session.

15. ***Possible problem:*** your dog may not settle at all, may repeatedly try to climb on you or get the food

    a. Have lower value treats.

    b. Try a different time of day.

    c. Shape any and all small signs of relaxation, such as a sit, or even a look away from you - but always place the food quietly on the floor between your dogs paws without engaging with them in any way, then sit back and relax again. Then you should gradually be able to build up to higher levels of relaxation with each session and more practise.

Building up the Duration of Settle

Once your dog can settle well and in different positions around your home when it's quiet, you can start to increase the time in between placing treats to extend the length of time they will remain calm and settled. Repeat the exercise the same way as before, but now we're going to add some challenges. As you add these challenges, remember to progress slowly, so repeat the exercise at count 10 until it's easy for your dog before progressing to count 15 etc.

Your Challenge list for Settle - Increasing Duration

Challenge: How long can you count...	Yep! My Dog Can Do That
Start off counting to 5 in between placing treats between your dogs paws	
Can you count to 10?	
Can you count to 15?	
Can you count to 20?	
Can you count to 30?	

Your Challenge List for Settle - Increasing Distractions

Once your dog can reliably self settle as soon as you do, you can start to add gradually increasing distractions to strengthen and embed the relaxed settle behaviour

NOTE: If you need to, you can increase the rate of reward when you add these challenges (make the time between rewards shorter again) to help your dog succeed. You could start by only counting to 1 or 2 between placing treats, then gradually increase to counting 3 if your dog is doing well, working your way back up to 5 and beyond, because your dog has already learnt the basics of the exercise, they usually progress quickly through new challenges.

Challenge: Can your dog remain settled...	Yep! My Dog Can Do That
When someone opens a door to the room & closes it again	
When someone walks into the room and out again - without engaging with you	
When someone walks into the room and talks to you briefly	
When you stand up and sit down again	
When you stand up, move to pick something up and sit down again	
Add your own challenges (but make them gradual in their distraction level)	

Again you want to keep these sessions short, 2-3 minutes or so, always ending calmly so your dog can remain relaxed following the exercise. Once your dog can remain settled for about a minute in between placing treats, is in a relaxed state even when there are some distractions, you can start to generalise the behaviour to other locations and outside.

Generalising the Behaviour to Other Locations & Outside (During Walks is the ideal time)

1. Choose a quiet area of a field or park, or choose a time of day when the location will be relatively quiet.

2. An ideal position could be something like a bench, slightly set back from foot traffic in a grassy area that will encourage your dog to lie down.

3. Repeat the exercise as you did at home. Settle yourself and relax, disengaging from your dog and when you see them start to relax, sit down or lie down, place a treat calmly between their paws.

4. Because you're now outside, even in a quiet location, there are more distractions for your dog, so any visible relaxation can be rewarded to begin to shape the settle behaviour. Even if they're standing quietly, calm & relaxed, you could place a treat between their paws. Remember to remain disengaged, just calmly place the treat.

5. You will want to reward quite frequently to start with, to maintain the relaxed state and help remind your dog of the exercise you have practised at home.

6. After 2-3 minutes of settle, calmly move off with a smile and continue your walk with an 'Ok Let's Go.'

7. Repeat the exercise several times throughout the course of your walk.

8. It's perfectly OK to increase and decrease the rate of reward as you need to each time you practise. This helps to provide the necessary communication and feedback to your dog, and will help them maintain their relaxed state with you in different situations and environments.

9. Over time the rate of reward can be reduced, and gradually your dog will start to choose to self settle whenever you settle, relax and disengage with them.

Teaching OVER

Why teach an 'Over' behaviour

- ✓ A useful management and control exercise to help reactive dogs
- ✓ Enables you to give your dog greater freedom by having greater control
- ✓ Makes it easier to manoeuvre your dog without pushing or pulling them around
- ✓ Makes it easy to get your dog to move out of the way of oncoming walkers / cyclists / traffic etc

'Over' in my personal opinion is a really useful communication to teach dogs, making it easier to give them clear instructions on where you want them to move to at any given time. The more detailed instructions that we teach our dogs to understand and respond to, the less need there is for us to push and pull them around, and the less chance they will make their own choices, which are often not the best ones, because they're simply not equipped to make those kind of decisions.

'Over' is an excellent exercise to have on cue for reactive dogs, because it gives you another positive behaviour to give your dog to focus on doing when you come across a trigger. You see the trigger at a distance ahead, and you know you need to manoeuvre your dog to a safe spot where you can wait or pass safely. So rather than try and drag your dog into an alleyway (creating tension) or behind a car, or into a driveway to give both of you the space you need, you can use 'Over', giving them a clear hand signal as to what that direction needs to be.

This exercise together with a previously taught 'Let's Go' and 'Touch', gives you a really strong communication tool, and when it comes to reactivity, for both the human and canine halves of the partnership, the less guesswork going on the better!

By having clear actionable strategies for emotionally charged situations (that have been previously rehearsed) the calmer and more efficient both yours and your dogs behaviours will be, leaving less and less room for those emotional eruptions.

The process for teaching over is very simple, as always you will need your tasty treat rewards in a pocket or treat bag, your dog on their normal length lead (4-6ft) and a safe walking space with room for you to move over to one side, preferably with little or no distractions to start with.

Ideal locations to teach and practise this might be

- ✓ Quiet country lanes with grass verges - having something to physically move over onto can be helpful for you both.

- ✓ Local parks or grassy areas where you can pick a quiet corner to walk up and down while you teach and practise.

- ✓ Quiet farm tracks wide enough for you to take several steps to the side, and ideally build up to 5 or 6 steps over.

Teaching OVER - Step by Step

1. As you walk along with your dog walking beside you, to begin with you're going to LURE your dog with a tasty treat.

2. So take out your tasty treat, show it to your dog, taking just one step to start with, move it away from them to the left or right, depending in which direction you're moving 'over'.

3. As they start to move sideways with you to follow the treat you say '<Fido> Over' and then follow with your CLICK/YESSS MARK and give them the treat.

4. Repeat this 5 or 6 times, always in the same direction to start with if you can.

5. Walk on a bit further, having some sniffy time, then repeat again for 3 or 4 treats.

6. Now you can dispense with the lure, and just use your hand, my hand signal for over is just my open hand out to the side, as if showing them where to go (like when teaching Touch, which it would be useful to have taught before this exercise) But to start with you could pretend you still have that tasty treat in your hand, to help your dog get it right during these learning stages, and then progress up to the open hand.

7. Repeat again with 3 or 4 treats, and then continue sniffy time.

8. Don't ask your dog for too many steps to the side to start with, just a couple to give them the idea, then you can build up the distance you cover with your 'Over' once they know what you mean.

9. Once your dog is doing well and immediately responding to your 'Over' request, then you can begin to increase how far you move over with them.

10. Make sure you give nice clear hand signals with this exercise, especially if you want to be able to use it when your dog is off lead.

11. You can also at this point start working on 'Over' in both directions. I tend to find this easier to teach by working in a quiet country lane with grass verges, and simply zig zagging down the lane working on each side, and therefore in each different direction.

12. Once your dog understands clearly the game of 'Over' you can start dropping it in randomly on your walks, but to start with, at times when you don't need it, remember you're both still learning.

13. Once you're getting fab responses, start testing out your new 'Over' manoeuvre in real life situations, but if your dog has triggers, there will be other foundation work you need to do prior to being able to use 'Over' effectively in these situations.

Your Challenge List for Over

Remember if any of these things are triggers for your dog, swap them out for something different and leave the triggers for now.

Challenge List: Can your dog move 'Over'	Yep! My Dog Can Do That!
On a quiet country lane when traffic comes	
When there is a person walking towards you	
When there is a cyclist coming toward you	
When there is a child on a bike/scooter	
When there is a group of people/children walking toward you	
When there is a person walking a dog coming toward you	

Challenge List: Can your dog move 'Over'	Yep! My Dog Can Do That!
Add your own challenges...	

Once your dog can do 'Over' really well, you can start practising it off lead, if they have a reliable recall and are good off lead. This will enable you to ask your dog to move over even if they're not right by your side at the time you ask them.

Teaching off lead 'Over' - Step by Step

1. You will need a fairly strong conditioned name response in place for this off lead exercise.

2. Go back to practising in very quiet non distracting locations.

3. Start off teaching the same way as before, when your dog is quite close to you.

4. Gradually build up the distance your dog is in front of you when you ask for your '<Fido> Over'.

5. Make sure you give nice clear hand signals with this exercise, so your dog knows and understands clearly what you're asking them to do.

6. You could also add a 'Sit' onto this, once your dog is over, again using hand signals, so once they have moved over, you can ask for a 'Sit' to hold them in place until you release them.

SECTION 3
Which Teaching Guides Do You Need and When

Whilst nothing is ever set in stone when it comes to teaching dogs, I have tried to compile the following protocols so that they will work more effectively by teaching each exercise in order. Having said that, of course everyone (human and canine) is different, and whilst I believe these teaching exercises are ordered to provide you with the most structured progress, if you find that switching things around works for you and your dog, then go right ahead and do that!

These lists are of course not the be all and end all to solving every dog related problem, it would be impossible to include all the information you need in a single book because there are so many variables involved, hence why working with an accredited force free professional teacher is always the best option if you're really struggling. Having said that, teaching and working on these exercises should certainly get you progressing in the right direction!

It can be helpful to note, that if you've been struggling with something for a while, it might be better to start back at the beginning and work through everything again, including the basics. It's often the case that once a problem is in place, there can be bad habits that have developed in both dogs and their people, but by starting back at the beginning, it can help you to notice and eliminate these habits as you go along.

In my personal experience, many of the clients I work with are missing the foundation exercises, the ones that create the engagement and basic responses, which is why the more difficult behaviours, things like great recall, being able to handle and improve reactivity, surviving the adolescent zone out period and being connected enough to walk nicely on a lead seem so much harder to achieve.

FOR DOGS THAT IGNORE YOU OR APPEAR DEAF
Teaching Your Dog to Listen to You More on Walks

1. Conditioned Name Response
2. Voluntary Check In
3. Voluntary Close
4. Proofed Sit
5. Loose Lead Walking - Foundation Exercises
6. This Way
7. Let's Go
8. Premack Recall

Surprisingly this is a hugely common complaint among guardians, their dog is a dream at home, but as soon as they get out on walks, they go deaf, it's like they zone out, nothing seems to get through. The most common reasons for this are because YOUR engagement with your dog only takes place when you NEED them to listen, in other words you don't interact with them enough at any other time, so they go off and find their own fun and completely disconnect from you. Whilst I'm not suggesting you spend all your walks constantly doing things with your dog, it's important that you periodically engage with them throughout your walk and not only when you NEED them to listen to you.

The other main reason this happens is because when you teach your dog behaviours you want them to do out on walks, you teach them the basics of the exercise, but then fail to follow through with your rehearsals out in the real world, with the type of distractions you're going to be competing against and the kinds of situations you really **need** your dog to respond in.

Make sure you follow through with all the engagement exercises so they become reliable in all situations and environments.

FOR DOGS THAT LACK SELF CONTROL
Teaching Your Dog They Can't Always Have the Things They Want

1. Lead Techniques
2. Proofed Sit
3. Voluntary Check In
4. Impulse Control
5. Conditioned Name Response
6. Leave It
7. Let's Go
8. Settle

If you have a dog that can be hyperactive, a bit demanding, a bit over zealous at times, unable to settle down and concentrate, especially in stimulating or distracting circumstances, then it may be that they have never learnt any self control.

The key to succeeding when teaching your dog self control exercises is to let them learn for themselves, if you do all their homework for them and keep prompting and asking for behaviours, they will never learn to either think for themselves or make choices based purely on consequences, which is essentially what self control is.

The definition of self control is: The ability to control ones emotions and desires, especially in difficult situations. Make sure you start out with easy levels of self control exercises and progressively increase the level of desire you present your dog with. If they can't make good choices at the easy levels, you're setting them up to fail if you progress to harder situations before they're ready.

FOR DOGS THAT PULL ON LEAD
Teaching Your Dog to Walk Nicely on the Lead

1. Lead Techniques
2. Voluntary Close
3. Conditioned Name Response
4. Voluntary Check In
5. Impulse Control
6. Loose Lead Walking - Foundation Exercises
7. Let's Go (adding this exercise into your lead walks gives you the opportunity to be unpredictably fun)

Teaching a dog to walk nicely on a loose lead requires plenty of patience and lots of consistency. Teaching a dog to stop pulling on a lead once they have learnt and practised that behaviour for some time, requires a lot more time, effort, patience and consistency.

The biggest help I can give you with this one is to separate your walks into free walks and teaching walks. Teaching walks are solely focused on lead work, integrated with 'sniffy time' breaks to relieve pressure on you both (but still no pulling). Teaching walks should be very short, take place in a very boring environment and if possible take place at least once every day, ideally a couple of times a day as it could help speed up progress.

Free walks ideally should be walks that you're able to put your dog straight into the car and drive to, thus eliminating the need to spend time doing lead training to get there, otherwise neither of you ever gets a break from practise, because the key to fast progress with lead work is consistency. If your dog has a good recall, you can simply let them off, if they don't have a good recall, have them on a long line so they can have some space to wander but without having to constantly do lead work exercises.

FOR DOGS THAT DON'T COME WHEN CALLED
Teaching Your Dog to Listen & Want to Run Back To You

1. Conditioned Name Response
2. Voluntary Check In
3. Lead Techniques
4. Recall Exercises & Games
5. Stop!
6. This Way
7. Touch
8. Leave It

Reliable recall is all about getting the foundation behaviours in place in the first instance. If you can't even get your dogs attention when you're out on a walk, the chances of you getting them to race back to you diminish greatly. Then it becomes all about motivation, and of course, again, rehearse, rehearse, rehearse! If you only ever call your dog back when you NEED to, you run the risk of setting them up to fail each time, and they can't learn anything from that.

Teach in stages, break it down into bitesize exercises and get each one working well individually before you put them all together. Think about it from your Dog's point of view what you're asking of them. When you recall them away from something it's actually 4 things you want, not just 1, you want them to:

1. Stop moving in the direction they're going
2. Disengage from whatever has interested them
3. Turn and re-engage with you
4. Run back to you

Which is potentially why recall is one of the biggest challenges for guardians to teach as a reliable behaviour. Most will say their dog is fine when there's nothing around, but as soon as there's a distraction, they fail to come back and that's because, at that point, it's become more than just a recall.

Most importantly, make all your recall exercises Big Fun! Be the most fun thing for your dog to hang out with, you're competing with some heavy duty interesting stuff. If you wander along in your own little world and they in theirs, you will miss engagement opportunities and they will become more disconnected from you. Let them know that you LOVE doing things with them on walks, but it has to be real, your dog will know if you're only pretending ☺

FOR DOGS THAT LIKE TO CHASE
Teaching Your Dog When They Can and Can't Chase Things

1. Conditioned Name Response
2. Voluntary Check In
3. Lead Techniques
4. Impulse Control
5. Premack Recall
6. Leave It
7. Let's Go

The biggest help I can give you with working to eliminate chase behaviours is to say, the process of learning plays a big part here.

- ✓ You have to have well rehearsed behaviours in place when you start to add in the 'trigger' situations.

- ✓ You have to actively seek out the trigger situations when you're fully set up to handle them, with the right rewards and controls in place, and rehearse A LOT again within those situations.

- ✓ You have to have your dog under control on a lead or long line to prevent them being able to free chase.

- ✓ You have to reward them with controlled chase in some way, in order to satisfy that need but keep it under your control and within your reward system.

FOR DOGS THAT LIKE TO JUMP UP
Teaching Your Dog How to Greet Politely

1. Conditioned Name Response
2. Hand Signals
3. Proofed Sit
4. Impulse Control
5. Settle

One of the key aspects of teaching your dog that it's a bit rude and inappropriate to jump up at people either in the home or out on walks is to make sure they can do it with you, members of your family, and people who are very familiar to them, before you start trying to stop them jumping up at visitors or strangers. If they can't respond to you in familiar situations, they're going to find it difficult to respond in situations where arousal/excitement/tension is higher. Lots of rehearsals and consistency needed with this one.

Another good approach for dogs that love to jump up, is to teach and put on cue a 'Jump up' behaviour. This can work really well because you can prevent your dog jumping at people who don't want to be jumped all over, but for those that do, you can actually reward your dog for sitting politely, by INVITING them (using their pre-taught cue) to jump up and go crazy with you. These kind of life rewards are very powerful reinforcers.

My Rommie Rescue dog Tramp loves this particular one! You can see him above in his polite sit, being invited to jump... and then throwing himself at me ☺ What a fun way to teach!

FOR DOGS THAT LIKE TO BARK A LOT
Teaching Your Dog They Don't Need to Bark Quite so Much

1. Conditioned Name Response
2. Leave It
3. Let's Go
4. Touch

In the first instance, you have to remember barking is what dogs do! Sorry I know that may be obvious, but when your dog is driving you mad with their barking, it can help to remember this is instinctive behaviour, and some are much more vocal than others, so may be worth bearing that in mind when you choose which breed of dog to share your life with.

If you have quite an intense barker, your first approach needs to be to find a way to reduce that intensity before you will be able to ask them to do an alternative behaviour. Whilst they're in 'crazy barking mode' they're unlikely to listen to anything you say.

You can do this by trying any of the following:

- Avoid shouting at them - you're just confirming that whatever they're barking at is indeed a cause for concern because you're getting worked up about it too.

- If you know when they're going to bark, say for example you know what time the postman comes each day, you could try having them on a lead with you at that time, away from the door, so when they hear that letterbox go, they will be further away from it giving you more opportunity to mark/reward them for hearing but not barking, or giving a little bark, you say 'Thank you' they look because THIS is new! ... and you can then mark/reward. Build up gradually moving closer and closer.

- You could try desensitizing them to the sound of the letterbox/doorbell by playing a recording at a low volume as you mark/reward for no barking. Gradually increase the volume. This doesn't work with all dogs, but it does with some.

- You could also try teaching them a behaviour you want, such as 'run to the kitchen' for which the cue is the letterbox, or someone knocking or the doorbell. You will have to teach & rehearse the behaviour many times first, then do controlled setups to associate this behaviour with the sounds at the door.

Once you have reduced the intensity of your dogs barking, you can then give them instructions on what you would prefer them to do, they will be more likely to respond because they're not so worked up, and then you can build and strengthen this new process.

Final note. Always thank your dog for letting you know there was 'something' there! After all, that is what they're doing, and by you acknowledging that, it can help them realise you're aware of the 'something' and you've said 'It's ok'. Although this in and of itself won't necessarily stop the barking, it can have a very positive impact on reducing intensity, which makes it easier for them to respond to alternative requests from you to do something different.

FOR DOGS THAT CAN BE REACTIVE ON WALKS
Helping Your Dog Feel Better in Situations They Feel Uncomfortable

1. Lead Techniques
2. Conditioned Name Response
3. Voluntary Check In
4. Loose Lead Walking - Foundation Exercises
5. Let's Go
6. Leave It
7. Touch
8. Over

Reactivity is such a complex issue, whether it be in the home or out on walks, it's obviously not possible to cover within the pages of this book, the kind of things that are going to solve that problem, but for reactive dogs, the more well known & well rehearsed behaviours they have to choose from, the easier it is for them NOT to default automatically to an emotional outburst.

Well rehearsed management manoeuvres, like Let's Go, Leave it, Over and Touch, can provide your dog with not only clear instructions of what to do in a tense situation, but also give them a sense of safety within your partnership. The lead techniques, loose lead walking and engagement exercises can ensure both you and your dog remain connected and able to communicate effectively, meaning you're able to guide them but without being heavy handed or adding tension to the situation.

Imagine you have an uncontrollable fear of flying, a situation in which your emotional reactions are difficult for you to control. Your partner who is travelling with you, is showing signs of anxiety, fear, uncertainty and struggles to maintain focus as you progress through all the check in and security procedures before boarding. What impact do you think this would have on your fears or anxiety?

Compare this to a partner who is calm, confident, unruffled and able to communicate clearly to you where you need to go, what you need to do, and gently but steadily guides you throughout the check in and security procedures and onwards to board the plane. What impact do you think this type of person would have on your fears or anxiety?

So although the exercises covered in this book are not a solution to reactivity, they're certainly an important part of the groundwork. They can provide you with a strong foundation from which you and your dog will become more connected and able to communicate with each other clearly, both of which are an essential part of a trusting relationship within which you're able to manage and reduce the intensity of reactive outbursts.

FINAL THOUGHTS

You don't know what you don't know. Many clients I work with are not lacking in their ability to teach their dogs the kinds of behaviours they want them to learn, they are simply lacking in some areas of knowledge and understanding because they've been approaching things from a human perspective instead of looking at them from the Dog's point of view.

If you're not a natural born dog teacher, then there are quite a lot of things here to learn and then remember to apply, and I get it, it can become pretty confusing at times and feel like there is just too much to know! Which is why I hope I have structured this learning process in such a way that makes it easier for you, as your dogs teacher, to progress through each stage systematically, which in turn helps you structure your dogs education in a way that makes it easy for you both to see steady but definite progress.

Enjoying the journey is something I cannot stress enough. Through all these exercises and challenges, you're building and strengthening the most amazing relationship that will bring you immense satisfaction and pleasure, but as with any relationship, it takes time. If you try to rush through to get to the end result, you miss out on some of the most important and pleasurable parts of the process, and may find the end result is not as good as you had hoped.

I can give you all the information, understanding and tools you need to achieve your desired outcome, but because this is a relationship, because this involves an emotional connection between two beings, I can't do it for you, the day to day application has to come from you.

If you put in the effort, the results you see will be quite simply... beautiful.

ABOUT THE AUTHOR

Meesh Masters is business owner at The Dog's Point of View and has enjoyed the great privilege of sharing the last 30 years of her life with many dogs of varying breeds, shapes and sizes. German Shepherds, Belgian Shepherds, Jack Russell Terriers, Border Collies and a variety of Mixed Breed dogs. She's also had the pleasure of working with a great many more over the last 15 years with her clients, and believes every single one teaches her something new.

She has a passion for not only canine psychology, but also human psychology and how the two are intertwined. Her journey as a trainer started around 20 years ago, when she needed help with a GSD rescue dog and some pretty extreme behavioural problems. After paying a lot of money to enlist the help of a behaviourist, was dismayed to find their approach was one of force, and a lack of empathy for the emotional wellbeing of her struggling dog. After asking them to leave, she started reading everything she could find, in an attempt to try to help her dog herself, and thus began taking courses and studying, and she hasn't stopped reading yet!

With a background in business and accounting, Meesh found when working with clients and their dogs that being able to provide clear, organised structure to what they were learning, helped them to stay on track and therefore be able to continually make progress without losing focus or motivation, and that was her inspiration to create practical step by step guides, books, courses and workbooks.

After becoming involved with Romanian Rescue dogs in 2015, both as a support advisor to new adopters and a fosterer herself, she was once again led to look deeper into the thinking, feeling, emotional depths of the dogs we spend our lives with. She began to realise how the Romanian dogs were different to British born dogs, how their genetics and bloodline, being from street dogs, meant they seemed to be more in tune with their instinctive nature's. She found she had to adjust the ways she interacted with and worked with these dogs, to accommodate their more streetwise and cautious characteristics. It became very evident that these dogs responded differently to 'training' in the conventional sense at times, and she found herself learning ways to bond more deeply, which led to the development of a greater understanding of the subtleties involved in truly listening to what our dogs tell us.

Meesh has diploma's in Advanced Canine Psychology and Life Coaching, has completed numerous courses with Dr Ian Dunbar, is a Reiki Master with Animal Reiki Certification and is a Member of the Pet Professional Guild British Isles. She currently lives in South Yorkshire with her Border Collie Sky and Romanian Rescue dog Tramp.

"Thank you for reading! If you enjoyed this book or found it useful I'd be very grateful if you'd post a short review on Amazon. Your support really does make a difference and I read all the reviews personally so I can get your feedback and make this and future books even better.

Thanks again for your support!"

LET'S WORK TOGETHER

If you would like help with your dogs training or behaviour, there are lots of ways we can work together. You can find all the details and information on the website at www.thedogspov.com

There will be online self paced courses and email courses being published very shortly, covering a range of topics, so be sure to subscribe on the website @www.thedogspov.com to receive notifications as these become available, if they're something you're interested in.

JOIN THE DOG's POINT OF VIEW COMMUNITY
We have tonnes of exciting stuff currently being developed, so remember to join the community to make sure you don't miss out on anything!

Find us on Facebook
The Dogs Point of View

Subscribe to the website @
http://thedogspov.com/

Subscribe to the YouTube Channel
The DOG's Point of View

APPENDIX

APPENDIX I

Essential Elements
Action Worksheet: HABITS

Using Your Habits Worksheet

- ☺ Take 10 minutes to review the Essential Elements #2 info, then sit down & create two lists.
- ☺ Write down anything your dog does that you would like to change or improve.
- ☺ Then next to it, write down any habits you can think of that YOU may be doing that trigger the behaviour or could be preventing it from improving.
- ☺ Then from your list, pick one habit to work on. Hint: **Pick the easiest one.**
- ☺ Work on changing only one habit at a time. It is said that trying to change more than one habit at a time significantly reduces the chance of success from 80% to 10%.

Your Dog's Behaviour	Your Current Behaviour

Your Dog's Behaviour	Your NEW Behaviour?

Some Easy Ways to Remind Yourself You Want to Change a Habit

Remember I said one of the hardest parts about changing a habit is remembering you want to be doing something different in the first place! Here are some ideas to help you remind yourself about the NEW behaviour you want to make a habit, you'll get the idea from this list and be able to change it up to fit what you're working on.

Behaviour you're working on	Possible Types of Reminders that might work well
Pulling on the lead	A post it note or coloured dot on the door you go out of A piece of coloured tape around your lead
Barking at Home	A brightly coloured tub of treats on the side A special toy to redirect to, left in a handy place
Jumping Up	A post it note or coloured dot on the door you come in through A coloured dot or piece of tape on your door keys
Begging for food	A funny poster on your fridge saying 'Ignore the begging dogs' A folded card you put out on the dinner table saying the same

One of the most powerful influences over your
dogs behaviour.... is your behaviour.
Rehearsal & Repetition Creates New Automated Habits in you both ☺

APPENDIX II

Essential Elements
Action Worksheet: THE BIG PICTURE

Remember, you don't want to be working on everything all at once, but it might be necessary to make sure you manage any minor problem behaviours for the time being, to make it easier to work on the bigger issues.

Put in the left hand column any major training or problem behaviours you're currently working on, or want to focus on. Then on the right hand side, make a note of any other less troublesome behaviours that could be having a negative impact on progress.

Main Behaviour Problem	Behaviours that could be having a negative impact
1. e.g. reactive when on lead	e.g. Also pulls on the lead
2.	
3.	

Work on or Manage?
Now from the list above, of 'Other Behaviours', make a note of what you want to work on if necessary, and which ones you will manage for the time being and how you're going to manage them.

Behaviour	Work on	Manage
e.g. Pulling on the lead	e.g. Spend 1 week intensively to solve this problem	e.g. Drive to walk area & put straight on long line.

APPENDIX III

Essential Elements
Action Worksheet: PRACTISE & REHEARSE

If you're working to teach your dog something new, or to change a behaviour like pulling on the lead or jumping up etc, then the basic process is usually more or less the same, with some tweaking here and there depending on what you're working on.

Make it Easy for Your Dog to Learn

'Learning' always takes place in the least distracting place, which is usually a quiet, familiar, boring room at home. Don't forget, once your dog has learnt the behaviour, it's just about rehearsing, so at each level they will hopefully progress quicker and quicker, because they already know the foundation of the exercise and have been reinforced for it.

Most people, do stage 1, then skip straight to stage 4 and then wonder why their dog struggles to get it right. As you can see, there's quite a few levels in between that need practising at, before your dog will be able to generalise the behaviour to any and all locations.

One more thing you need to know about practise...

Dog's Learn Best & Quickest
With the Most Repetitions in the Least Amount of Time

So what I mean by that, is not that your dog will learn best & quickest if you practise constantly all day every day, hammering home the education, that will just end up in misery for you both!

What I mean is, that little short regular teaching sessions a few times every day, or integrated into daily life, will help your dog to progress quicker, than if you practise a couple times on Monday, then don't do any again 'til Thursday or Friday, then maybe do some again on Sunday, when you remember. This dispersed kind of practise will take your dog longer to learn, so be aware of that and cut them some slack if they don't seem to be picking it up quickly.

To quickly recap the learning levels

Level 1 - AT HOME
1. Learn the mechanics of the behaviour at home in non distracting environment.
2. Put a cue word to the behaviour.
3. Practise in different rooms around the home with varying levels of distraction.

Level 2 - IN THE GARDEN
1. Practise in the garden or just outside your home.
2. Practise in the garden with varying levels of distraction.

Level 3 - LOW LEVEL DISTRACTION AREAS
1. Practise on quiet familiar walks.

2. Practise prior to high level arousal situations e.g. going out to the garden, going for a walk, getting in the car, prior to being allowed to greet visitors.

3. Generalise to all everyday familiar walks, including parks, fields and street walks.

Remember, if you find your dog is very distracted when you first move up to more distracting locations, try staying in one place for a moment, or moving back and forth over a short area (depending on what it is you're working on) to allow your dog to acclimatise before asking them to focus & practise. If you always keep moving forward, your dog is being flooded with new information (sights, sounds, smells) which makes it hard for them to concentrate and learn.

Remember, practise, chill out, sniff, wander, practise, chill out, sniff, wander, play and so on, keep everything in balance and fun ☺

Level 4 - HIGH LEVEL DISTRACTION AREAS

Now you can start to practise in gradually more distracting places, building up to being able to take your dog into the EXACT situation you NEED that behaviour to work in, then REHEARSE SOME MORE, then test it out. So if it's recall away from other dogs, you need to practise recalling away from other dogs, until your dog is clearly good at it, and choosing happily to come to you, because if they're not doing it happily, as soon as you take that training line off, there's a fair chance they won't choose you.

1. Practise in a busier walk location, perhaps where there are more people, more dogs, more traffic.

2. Practise in highly distracting environments if required. Town Centres, other people's houses, dog parks.

3. Practise in situations that your particular dog finds exciting e.g. other dogs playing/children playing/local football match.

4. Practise in situations that your dog finds highly arousing e.g. dinner time/people eating/busy road locations

5. Teach & practise when your dog is a distance away from you (if appropriate for the exercise you're working on)

6. Teach & practise for your dog to maintain the behaviour for slightly longer amounts of time (if appropriate for the exercise)

Remember, if your dog is really distracted and unable to concentrate when you first start teaching in high distraction locations, stay on the outskirts for a little while, and gradually move closer as your dog settles. Just pay attention to stress levels if these types of environments are something that causes your dog to become anxious. Better to go slower in baby steps, than too fast and push your dog completely out of their comfort zone. That could leave a lasting negative impact, which we definitely don't want!

So to help you stay on track you could use something like the following teaching record:

TEACHING RECORD

Behaviour	*Example - SIT*			
Cue (Word)	*Sit*			
Cue (Visual)	*Lift hand to chest*			
Level 1 At Home	*99% will respond*			
Level 2 In the Garden	*95% will respond*			
Level 3 Low Distraction	*75% will respond*			
Level 4 High Distraction				
Duration	-			
Distance (Maintain)	-			
Distance (Respond)	*10ft @ home only*			

(NB: You won't necessarily use all of these for all behaviours)

Points to Remember

✓ If your dog is failing, you have most likely moved too quickly (or may not be using the right level of reward in relation to difficulty of exercise)

✓ Have fun! Make your training sessions fun for you both, after all, life is just a game! Remember as a kid that teacher you loved who made learning fun, BE that teacher ☺

✓ You can't solve a problem within the situation the problem exists. You need to practise at times OTHER than when you NEED your dog to respond, to teach them, to strengthen them, to embed the behaviours. Just randomly practise. With things like recall this can also help prevent accidental cues developing, whereby you recall your dog, and that actually CUES them to look for something you're calling them away from.

Another Useful Record

Something else I've found useful for my clients, to help them keep on track with teaching and prevent them feeling overwhelmed, is to recommend they only practise one exercise at a time on each walk. I have a little planner I share with them to help remind them of what they want to be focusing on each day, so everything gets covered. There's plenty of variety, no one gets bored and they don't have to keep remembering.

I thought you might find it useful too, so I have put a copy here. I've included a blank copy for you to use, or you could draw something similar on a wipe board or sheet of paper, if this is the kind of thing that would be helpful for you.

Example Daily Practise Record

DAY	AM WALK	PM WALK
Monday	Let's go	Touch
Tuesday	Name Game	Let's go
Wednesday	Touch	Recall
Thursday	Let's go	Touch
Friday	Name Game	Let's go
Saturday	Recall	Name Game
Sunday	Let's go	Touch

Your Daily Practise Record

DAY	AM WALK	PM WALK
Monday		
Tuesday		
Wednesday		
Thursday		
Friday		
Saturday		
Sunday		

Always Remember To High Five Your Daily Wins!

It can be all too easy to see only what's 'wrong'... When before your very eyes there are so many things that are Right!

The Dog's Point of View
www.thedogspov.com
Photography: Jonathan Hall

References

https://www.psychologytoday.com/us/blog/canine-corner/201606/are-voice-commands-or-hand-signals-more-effective-dogs

Tellington Touch - www.tteam-ttouch.com

Susan Garrett - www.susangarrett.com

Resources

PDF Download of Tables & Challenge Lists

If you would like a basic PDF download of all the tables and challenge lists for printing purposes or if you have multiple dogs in the household, please contact me via the website at www.thedogspov.com.

Recommended Websites

Grisha Stewart - www.grishastewart.com

Dr Ian Dunbar - www.dunbaracademy.com

Relationship Centred Dog Training by Suzanne Clothier - www.suzanneclothier.com

Patricia McConnell - www.patriciamcconnell.com

CARE for Reactive Dogs - www.careforreactivedogs.com

Find a Force Free Teacher

The Pet Professional Guild British Isles (PPGBI) - www.ppgbi.com

The Institute of Modern Dog Trainers (IMDT) - www.imdt.uk.com

The International Companion Animal Network (ICAN) - www.companionanimal.network

The International Association of Animal Behaviour Consultants - www.iaabc.org

The Victoria Stillwell Academy - www.vsdogtrainingacademy.com

The Pet Professional Network (PPN) - www.petpronetwork.co.uk (Website going live Aug/Sep 2018)

The Association of Pet Behaviour Counsellors - www.apbc.org.uk

The Association of Pet Dog Trainers - www.apdt.co.uk

Recommended YouTube Channels

Zak George

Dog Training by Kikopup

Urban Dawgs

School of Canine Science (Nando Brown & Jo-Rosie Haffenden)

Kristen Crestejo

Domesticated Manners (Chirag Patel)

Training Positive

DogStarDaily (Dr Ian Dunbar)

Printed in Great Britain
by Amazon

28622274R00086